Pleasures

of the

Palettes

FINE FOOD AND FINE ART

Production Coordination:
Bobbi Jo Haynes Kamnitzer and Kirsten Ross

Text Editor and Artist/Chef Biography Writer:
Donald Downes

**GOLDEN
WEST** ☼
PUBLISHERS

Cover photo by Bob Carey. Food styling by Bobbi Jo and Razz Kamnitzer.

Printed in the United States of America

ISBN #1-885590-22-9

Golden West Publishers, Inc.
4113 N. Longview Ave.
Phoenix, AZ 85014, USA
(602) 265-4392

Pleasures of the *Palettes*

for the benefit of the

Center Against Sexual Abuse (CASA)

presented by:

THE PHOENICIAN
SCOTTSDALE

and

Ed Mell ♦ *"Shifting Storm"*

Acrylic on Canvas   30" x 30"

Pleasures of the Palettes is an annual culinary and art event which benefits the Center Against Sexual Abuse (CASA). In the spirit of creativity and expression, renowned contemporary artists and accomplished culinary masters from all over the country gather in the Valley of the Sun to volunteer their talents to benefit CASA's violence prevention and counseling programs. CASA is the only nonprofit agency in Maricopa County, Arizona dedicated to preventing violence in all its forms, particularly sexual abuse.

At the *Pleasures of the Palettes* reception and art sale, the artists' work is sold to benefit CASA. At the event dinner, chefs create culinary masterpieces for the art patrons. Following dinner, the guests, artists and chefs interact in creating works of art.

Pleasures of the Palettes and Golden West Publishers are proud to present this Art/Cookbook, featuring exquisite recipes from all of the participating chefs as well as the intriguing art images created by the participating artists.

Proceeds from this publication benefit the Center Against Sexual Abuse.

Thank you for your support.

This book is dedicated to the emotional, physical and spiritual well-being of children and families everywhere.

Elias Rivera ✦ *"Solola Pots"*

Oil on Linen   80" x 68"

Pleasures of the *Palettes*

— Sponsors —

AAARDVARK AARMADILLO
AMERICA WEST AIRLINES
AMERICAN EXPRESS
THE ARIZONA BUSINESS JOURNAL
ART HANDLERS, FINE ART SERVICES
ART SOLUTIONS
BUTLER DESIGN GROUP
deCOMPRESSION GALLERY
DEL WEBB/TERRAVITA CORPORATION
EMS - EQUIPMENT MAINTENANCE SERVICES, INC.
GOLDEN WEST PUBLISHERS, INC.
DR. AND MRS. ANTHONY HEDLEY
JEWELRY BY GAUTHIÉR
KILFOYLE, BRUNER & KETTELL, L.L.C.
LA SALLE PARTNERS
MARISCAL, WEEKS, MCINTYRE & FRIEDLANDER, P.A. - GARY L. BIRNBAUM
MEAKER THE PRINTER
NORWEST BANK ARIZONA
NORTH PHOENIX HEART CENTER
OPUS SOUTHWEST CORPORATION
THE PHOENICIAN
ROSS BROWN PARTNERS
SALT RIVER PROJECT
SNELL & WILMER, L.L.P.
STREICH LANG
SUPER SHUTTLE
MR. AND MRS. PETER THOMAS
TIMBERLINE PRODUCTIONS
DR. AND MRS. DELWYN WORTHINGTON
WELLS FARGO BANK

HOTEL ACCOMMODATIONS

BEST WESTERN EXECUTIVE PARK
DOUBLETREE GUEST SUITES
FIESTA INN
HILTON SUITES
HOLIDAY INN MIDTOWN
THE LEXINGTON HOTEL
RAMADA INN AIRPORT

Gustavo Ramos Rivera ✦ *"Flor de los Sueños"*
Oil on Canvas   60" x 60"

Acknowledgments

"The only thing that can save the world is the reclaiming of the awareness of the world."

— Alan Ginsburg

Pleasures of the Palettes wishes to thank those of you who lend your time, energy, creativity and resources to this project and its important cause...

To all of our participating artists and chefs, thank you for lending stellar recognition to this event and for your dedication to the "reclaiming of the awareness of the world."

We are extremely grateful to The Phoenician Management team: Mr. Alan Fuerstman, Managing Director, Mr. Ian Reid, Director of Food and Beverage, Mr. Charles Stuart, Chef Eric Laqua and Chef James Cohen. Through their generosity and commitment to our community, **Pleasures of the Palettes** is allowed to take place at The Phoenician and enjoy its world class service and surroundings.

To America West Airlines, we thank you for your continued VIP treatment of our incoming special guests and participants and to all of our event Sponsors...our sincere appreciation for your support.

To Andra and Mitchell Prager, along with all of the individual hotels and resorts donating rooms to visiting artists, chefs and special guests, our utmost appreciation for your continued generosity.

Our most sincere thanks to Steve Finch and Brent Turley, owners of El Estribo Lodge, for inviting us into their spectacular historical home and hosting "Le Roti"...our artist and chef welcome party, which in itself raises funds for CASA, with over 400 guests in attendance. We would also like to recognize and thank Libby Cohen, Chairperson for "Le Roti," Casa Connection and everyone involved in putting on this event.

Thanks to Super Shuttle for providing superior ground transportation to all of our visiting participants.

To Timberline Productions, along with John Gibbons and the entire technical staff at The Phoenician, thanks for all the video and audio production support...you make us look good!

For their various areas of vital assistance, our special thanks to: Tom Meaker - Meaker the Printer, Rebecca Reeves - Rebecca Reeves Public Relations, John Armstrong - Armstrong/Prior, Montague & Company Marketing Communications, Bob Carey and Marsha Bruner.

Thank you, Sharon and Chelle Pattison of Art Handlers and Art Solutions for expertly taking on the huge responsibility of collecting, delivering and displaying the works of art we so proudly present.

To the entire CASA Board of Directors and Staff, thank you for your continued support of this event and for being the true champions of this cause. We would also like to acknowledge and thank all of our volunteers whose assistance at **Pleasures of the Palettes** is crucial.

Heartfelt appreciation to Stephanie Orr, Executive Director of the Center Against Sexual Abuse, for her enormous efforts, superb diplomacy and unfaltering belief in this event from its inception. We've come a *long* way, Steph!

To Donald Downes (writer extraordinaire!), thank you for all your hard work in creating this book [read more about Donald on page 144].

Our sincere gratitude to Lee and Bruce Fischer and all of you at Golden West Publishers; your support and enthusiasm for this publication have been a godsend...

And finally, loving thanks to Rudy, Razz and Lance.

Kirsten Ross and Bobbi Jo Haynes Kamnitzer

Pleasures of the Palettes, 1997

Table of Contents

APPETIZERS

ENTREES

Table of Contents — Entrees (continued)

DESSERTS

PARTICIPATING ARTISTS

Carlos Aguilar Linares — *Mexico City, Mexico*

John Armstrong — *Phoenix, Arizona*

Bill Barrett — *New York, New York*

John Battenberg — *San Francisco, California*

Larry Bell — *Taos, New Mexico*

David Bierk — *Peterborough, Ontario, Canada*

David Bradley — *Santa Fe, New Mexico*

Stephen Britko — *Santa Fe, New Mexico*

Anne Coe — *Apache Junction, Arizona*

Thomas Coffin — *Phoenix, Arizona*

Joel Coplin — *Mesa, Arizona*

Philip C. Curtis — *Scottsdale, Arizona*

Marc Jasper D'Ambrosi — *Tempe, Arizona*

John Dawson — *Phoenix, Arizona*

Karl Dowhie — *Tempe, Arizona*

John Edwards — *London, England*

Bella Feldman — *San Francisco, California*

Rudy Fernandez — *Phoenix, Arizona*

Douglas Kent Hall — *Alcalde, New Mexico*

James Havard — *Santa Fe, New Mexico*

James Holmes — *Santa Fe, New Mexico*

Kevin Irvin — *Phoenix, Arizona*

Kathryn Jacobi — *Santa Monica, California*

Kathryn Kain — *San Francisco, California*

Mayme Kratz — *Phoenix, Arizona*

Earl Linderman — *Scottsdale, Arizona*

Lyle London — *Scottsdale, Arizona*

Francisco Lopez (OCHOA) — *Gallup, New Mexico*

Merrill Mahaffey — *Santa Fe, New Mexico*

Michael Marlowe — *Phoenix, Arizona*

Mario Romero Mauricio — *Mexico City, Mexico*

Buck McCain — *Eagar, Arizona*

Mark McDowell — *Scottsdale, Arizona*

Ed Mell — *Phoenix, Arizona*

Jesús Bautista Moroles — *Rockport, Texas*

Tom Ortega — *Phoenix, Arizona*

Thomas A. Philabaum — *Tucson, Arizona*

Howard Post — *Mesa, Arizona*

Otto Rigan — *Phoenix, Arizona*

Elias Rivera — *Santa Fe, New Mexico*

Gustavo Ramos Rivera — *San Francisco, California*

Mel Roman — *Scottsdale, Arizona*

Paul Sarkisian — *Santa Fe, New Mexico*

Bill Schenck — *Apache Junction, Arizona*

Fritz Scholder — *Scottsdale, Arizona*

Kevin Sloan — *Key West, Florida*

Joe Willie Smith — *Phoenix, Arizona*

Mark Spencer — *Santa Fe, New Mexico*

Beth Ames Swartz — *Scottsdale, Arizona*

Aung Aung Taik — *San Francisco, California*

Bob "Daddy-O" Wade — *Austin, Texas*

Edward "Rusty" Walker — *Chandler, Arizona*

Masoud Yasami — *Scottsdale, Arizona*

Artist Image Index, page 143

APPETIZERS

Food styling -- Bobbi Jo & Razz Kamnitzer *Photography -- Bob Carey*

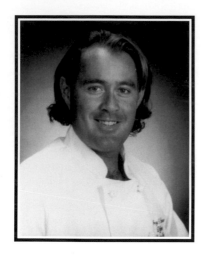

Jeffrey Beeson

Jeffrey Beeson *began his cooking career at home in the kitchen of his parents, both of whom enjoyed cooking. He worked his way through college doing many different jobs at local ethnic eateries and realized cooking was for him. After graduating from the University of Oregon, Jeffrey delved into cooking, voraciously reading cooking books and learning skills from some of the country's top chefs. His culinary addresses include Top of the Rock at The Buttes, Tempe, Arizona; and Camelview Radisson Resort and Windows on the Green at The Phoenician Resort, both in Scottsdale, Arizona.*

Jeffrey joined The Pointe Hilton Resorts as chef de cuisine of Different Pointe of View in 1995. His regional American cuisine reflects both classical and current cooking techniques as well as utilizing ingredients and products indigenous to the Southwest. When not in the resort's kitchen, Jeffrey enjoys spending time with Nora, his wife, and their new baby daughter, Sydnee, and an occasional rock climbing or biking outing.

Lobster and Roasted Corn Tamales

Makes 4 Tamales

- 4 ounces lobster meat
- 1 1/2 ounces roasted corn kernels
- 6 ounces tamale masa mix
- 1 tablespoon chopped onion
- 1 teaspoon minced garlic
- 1 tablespoon olive oil
- 1 tablespoon chopped cilantro
- 4 large corn husks, softened in water, patted dry
- Kosher salt and cracked black pepper to taste
- Cilantro sprigs for garnish

Avocado Salsa:

- 1 avocado, peeled and diced
- 1 teaspoon chopped poblano chile
- 1 teaspoon chopped red onion
- 1 teaspoon chopped red bell pepper
- 1 teaspoon lime juice
- Kosher salt and cracked pepper to taste

Pico de Gallo (fresh salsa):

- 1 cup chopped tomato
- 1 tablespoon diced red onion
- 1 tablespoon diced yellow onion
- 1 tablespoon diced green onion
- 1 tablespoon chopped cilantro
- 1 tablespoon diced poblano chile
- 1 teaspoon corn oil
- 1 tablespoon jalapeño Tabasco®
- 1 tablespoon lime juice

1. Prepare pico de gallo: Combine all ingredients in a bowl. Set aside.

2. Prepare avocado salsa: Combine all ingredients in a bowl. Set aside.

3. Prepare lobster tamales: Sauté lobster meat, corn kernels, onions, and garlic in olive oil until cooked and soft; stir in cilantro and allow to cool.

4. Flatten 1 1/2 ounces tamale masa mix in corn husk until 1/4-inch thick. Place lobster mixture in the middle of masa and fold (like an envelope) to form tamale. Repeat with remaining ingredients. Steam for 45 minutes.

5. Place tamales on plates and garnish with sprigs of cilantro; serve with avocado salsa and pico de gallo.

Lobster Cakes

Makes 4 Servings

    4 live Maine lobsters, 1 1/2 pounds each, poached and meat
        removed
    4 cups cream
    8 teaspoons chopped chives
    2 teaspoons sea salt
    1/2 teaspoon freshly ground black pepper
    4 teaspoons fresh lemon juice
    2 cups brioche bread crumbs
    2 lightly beaten eggs
    1/4 cup clarified butter

Rémoulade Sauce:

    1 1/2 cups mayonnaise
    1 1/2 teaspoons Dijon mustard
    2 tablespoons chopped dill pickle
    2 tablespoons capers
    2 tablespoons chopped fresh parsley
    2 tablespoons chopped fresh chervil

1. Prepare rémoulade sauce: Combine all ingredients in a blender; blend until smooth. Refrigerate for at least two hours to allow flavors to blend.

2. Prepare lobster cakes: Chop the lobster meat into medium dice and place in a mixing bowl. Place the cream in a pan and reduce by 2/3. Mix the chives, salt, pepper, lemon juice, half of the breadcrumbs, eggs and reduced cream with the lobster meat. Form into small cakes and dust with the remaining bread crumbs.

3. Sauté in clarified butter until golden brown on both sides. Serve cakes with rémoulade sauce.

James Cohen

James Cohen *majored in photography in college. "I actually started cooking in order to pay for my photographic equipment," he remarks. His discovery of fine foods, however, led him to the Culinary Institute of America.*

James' cooking career has included stopovers at The Colony Square Hotel in Atlanta and the Denver Country Club. Also in Denver, he was chef and owner of Plum Tree Caterers and Cafe. While working at Denver's famous Tante Louise restaurant, James drew the attention of Julia Child, who featured him in her PBS series "Dining with Julia."

Before becoming The Phoenician's executive chef in mid-1996, James headed the kitchens of The Wildflower at the Lodge at Vail, Vail, Colorado. Under his direction the restaurant received awards for its creative American cuisine from "Travel Holiday" and "DiRoNA" (Distinguished Restaurants of North America), as well as recognition from the James Beard Foundation.

Sanford

D'Amato *graduated from the Culinary Institute of America in 1974. He completed a one-year fellowship in the Escoffier Room and cooked at various New York City restaurants throughout the 1970s. In 1980, Sanford returned home to Milwaukee's John Byron's restaurant where he received national acclaim in 1985 as one of "Food & Wine's Top 25 Hot New Chefs" and "Bon Appetit," in a 1988 feature, recognized him as "one of the finest seafood chefs in the country." Sanford received gold medals in the 1988 and 1989 American Seafood Challenge and was among the twelve chefs personally selected by Julia Child to cook for her 80th birthday celebration in 1988.*

In 1989, Sanford and his wife, Angela, opened Sanford Restaurant. It has received accolades in "Esquire," "Food & Wine," "Bon Appetit," "Wine Spectator" and the "Chicago Tribune." Nominated for six consecutive years, the James Beard Foundation awarded Sanford America's Best Chef: Midwest in 1996. In 1995 the restaurant received Four Diamond recognition from AAA, and Mobil Travel Guide bestowed Sanford Restaurant its Four-Star award in January of 1997.

Chilled Saffron Mussel Soup
with Grilled Asparagus

Makes 8 Servings

  4 tablespoons olive oil, divided use
  1 ounce shallot, diced
  1 1/2 ounces garlic, sliced
  10 parsley stems
  3 sprigs thyme
  3 bay leaves
  1 1/2 teaspoons black peppercorns, crushed
  1 quart white wine
  5 pounds mussels
  2 cups chicken stock
  1 tablespoon saffron
  2 cups cream
  16 medium asparagus, cleaned and blanched crisp, save
     trimmings

1. Prepare the soup: Add 3 tablespoons olive oil to a stainless pot. Add asparagus trimmings, shallots and garlic; sauté one minute. Add spices and herbs; toss. Add mussels and wine. Cover and steam 5 to 6 minutes. Turn mussels over and steam another five minutes until mussels open. Drain, reserving stock; clean mussels. Chill mussels covered.

2. Strain reserved stock into a stainless pot. Add chicken stock and saffron and bring to a boil. Cover and infuse 1/2 hour. Chill and finish with cream.

3. Prepare asparagus: Toss asparagus with remaining olive oil and salt and pepper; grill.

4. Divide asparagus and mussels among 8 serving bowls. Ladle soup over and serve.

Parmesan Pudding with Sweet Pea Sauce

Makes 6 to 8 Servings

- 1 tablespoon unsalted butter
- 2 tablespoons all-purpose flour
- 3/4 cup light cream
- 3/4 cup whole milk
- 3/4 cup heavy cream
- 1 large egg
- 2 large egg yolks
- 2/3 cup finely grated Parmesan cheese
- 1/4 teaspoon kosher salt
- 1/8 teaspoon black pepper

Sweet Pea Sauce:

- 1 1/2 cups fresh or defrosted frozen sweet peas
- 3/4 cup chicken broth or canned low-sodium chicken broth
- 3 tablespoons heavy cream
- 1/4 teaspoon kosher salt
- 1/8 teaspoon black pepper
- Pea shoots, for garnish (optional)

1. Preheat the oven to 250 degrees. Butter a miniature (3x6) bread pan and line it with parchment paper.

2. Melt the butter in a medium-size saucepan; whisk in the flour. Continue whisking until the mixture is bubbling and has the consistency of mashed potatoes. Slowly whisk in the light cream.

3. Turn off the heat, slowly add the milk, heavy cream, egg and egg yolks, whisking well after each addition. Add the Parmesan, stirring until fully incorporated. Stir in the salt and pepper.

4. Pour the pudding into the prepared pan; place the pan in a larger pan filled with enough water to come halfway up the sides of the bread pan. Cover with aluminum foil, gently place in the oven, and bake for about 2 hours. Pudding will be somewhat firm and a knife inserted in the center will come out clean. Let cool; cover and refrigerate overnight.

5. Prepare the pea sauce: Place the peas, chicken broth, cream, salt and pepper in a blender and blend until smooth. Place the sauce in a small saucepan over very low heat and cook until warm, about 1 to 2 minutes. Pea sauce can be made ahead, covered and refrigerated.

6. Assembly: Unmold the pudding onto a cutting board. Cut into 6 to 8 slices and place each slice in the center of a heatproof plate. Place the plate in the oven and heat until the pudding is just warm, about 2 to 3 minutes. Pour the sauce around the pudding slices and garnish with the pea tendrils, if desired.

Todd English *began his cooking career at an early age like many of his peers. After graduating with honors from the Culinary Institute of America, he practiced his craft at New York's La Cote Basque, with Jean Jacques Rachou.*

He then traveled to Italy where he apprenticed at two fine restaurants: Dal Pescatore, in Canto Sull O'lio, and Paraccuchi, in Locando D'Angello. Todd credits his time spent in Italy with the development of his cooking style and approach to food. After returning to the States, he opened Michela's and was its executive chef for three years.

Todd is currently chef and owner of Olives as well as Figs, a pizzeria, in Charlestown, Boston and Wellesley, Massachusetts. Olives, which Todd opened in April of 1989 with Olivia, his wife, has been voted one of the Top Ten Restaurants by "Esquire" magazine and has received laudatory ink in "Bon Appetit," "Food & Wine" and "The New York Times." Todd can be seen on the Discovery Channel's "Great Chefs of the Northeast" cooking series. His new book, "The Olives' Table" (Simon & Schuster), is due out mid-1997.

Todd English — **Olives** *— Charlestown, Massachusetts*

Kevin Gay

Kevin **Gay** *has been in and around kitchens since he was fourteen years old. His hands-on culinary education has led to such cooking addresses as the Snowshoe Ski Resort in West Virginia and The Lodge at Vail, Vail, Colorado. Kevin joined The Phoenician as sous chef of The Terrace restaurant in 1995. In 1996, he was appointed chef de cuisine of The Terrace.*

Kevin has traveled and worked in hotels and small, family-owned restaurants in many Italian regions, including Liguria, Piedmont, Tuscany and Umbria. It's no wonder he includes "great Italian food" as a favorite, along with grilled food. "I love food from the grill," he says.

When not in the kitchen, Kevin says he enjoys snow skiing, mountain biking and reading cookbooks.

Seared Foie Gras with Honey-Port Vinaigrette

Makes 4 Servings
4 Mission figs
1 cup port wine
12 ounces foie gras, cut into 1/2-inch thick slices
12 ounces arugula, cleaned
2 tablespoons dry vermouth
Salt and pepper to taste

Honey-Port Vinaigrette:
1 tablespoon chopped thyme
1 tablespoon champagne wine vinegar
1/2 cup honey
1 cup extra-virgin olive oil
Salt and pepper to taste

1. Poach the figs in the port wine until soft. Strain liquid and reduce to a syrup; reserve for vinaigrette. Cool and quarter figs.

2. Prepare vinaigrette: In a small bowl combine thyme, vinegar, 1 tablespoon reduced port and honey. Add olive oil, whisking until emulsified and very thick. Season and set aside.

3. Prepare the foie gras: Heat a large sauté pan until it is very hot. Sear foie gras slices on both sides until tender. Remove foie gras to a plate and reserve the rendered fat. Sauté arugula with rendered fat until wilted. Deglaze with vermouth. Season and remove from heat.

5. Arrange arugula on plates. Place foie gras slices on top. Drizzle the plate with vinaigrette and garnish with figs.

Maine Crab Risotto

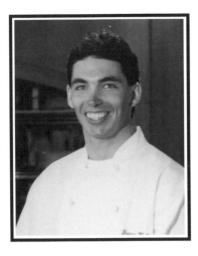

Makes 4 Servings
    4 ounces arborio rice
    1 1/2 ounces butter
    1/2 ounce olive oil
    1 ounce small dice onion
    1/2 tablespoon chopped garlic
    3 ounces white wine
    3 cups fish stock, hot
    6 ounces Maine crab, picked over
    2 tablespoons chopped chives
    Salt and pepper to taste
    1 1/2 tablespoons fresh lemon juice

Chive Oil:
    1 1/2 ounces chives
    1/2 cup olive oil

Fried Leeks:
    2 ounces leeks, julienne
    Cornstarch
    Vegetable oil for frying

1. Prepare the chive oil: Blanch the chives in boiling water for 20 seconds and shock in ice water. Remove from water and pat dry with paper towels. Place the chives in a blender along with the oil and blend until chives are emulsified. Place into a small stainless steel pot and cook while stirring with a wooden spoon. Bring to a simmer for 2 minutes and strain through a cheesecloth. Cool and set aside until needed.

2. Prepare fried leeks: Dust leeks with cornstarch. Fry in 350 degree peanut oil for 45 seconds. Remove to paper towels to drain.

3. Heat 1/2 ounce of butter and 1/2 ounce of olive oil in a small saucepot. Add the onions and cook until translucent. Add the garlic and cook for 30 seconds. Add the rice and stir with a wooden spoon. Add the white wine and stir until the wine is almost gone.

4. Ladle stock into pot to almost cover the rice; stir until the stock is absorbed into the rice. Repeat procedure, using all the stock. Stir in remaining butter, crab, chives; season to taste with salt and pepper.

5. Place finished risotto on plates and garnish each with 1/2 ounce of chive oil and fried leeks.

Tom Gay

Tom Gay *has always had his sights set on cooking professionally. He began his culinary career as a line cook at The Fireplace Restaurant in his home town of Paramus, New Jersey.*

A graduate of the Culinary Institute of America, Tom's cooking experience includes working with George Marone of Aqua, a renowned San Francisco specialty seafood eatery. He has been with The Lodge at Vail, an Orient Express Hotel, for more than five years. During his stay, he has fine-tuned his cooking talents through European travel and training at other Orient Express properties in Italy: Hotel Cipriani, Venice; Villa San Michele, Florence; and Hotel Splendido, Portofino.

Being at a mountain resort, Tom's time out of the kitchen is spent skiing in the winter and mountain biking and golfing in the summer. Foie gras ranks tops among his favorite foods, and had he not become a chef, Tom says he might have gone into carpentry or furniture making.

Stephen

Kalt *was supposed to be a doctor. He says his parents still wonder why he's not been to medical school. After Stephen graduated from the University of Florida with a degree in business administration, he moved to Tennessee and developed a small chain of eateries titled The Best Italian Restaurant. He sold his interest in the restaurants in 1985, returned to New York and worked in such prestigious kitchens as Le Cirque, Arcadia, Humbert's and Rakel.*

In 1992, he formed Stephen Kalt Associates, which specialized in food, service, systems and design. Recently, he has been responsible for such successful projects as Main Street, Kelley and Ping, Fresco, Park Avalon, Central Market, Hot and Crusty Bakery, as well as his own restaurant, Spartina. Stephen plays guitar and piano and has a fascination for the history of food.

Seared Tuna Tartare with Pomegranate Molasses and Curry Oil

Makes 6 Servings

    1 pound fresh, clean sushi-grade tuna
    4 teaspoons finely diced red bell pepper
    4 teaspoons finely diced poblano chile
    6 tablespoons virgin olive oil
    3 tablespoons fresh lime juice
    Salt and pepper
    2 ounces crème fraîche (sour cream can be substituted)
    2 medium endive, julienne
    6-8 chive spears
    2 tablespoons extra-virgin olive oil
    1 tablespoon sherry vinegar

Curry Oil:
    3 tablespoons curry powder
    4 ounces vegetable oil

Pomegranate Molasses:
    8 ounces pomegranate juice

1. Prepare curry oil: Combine curry powder and oil; let stand for 24 hours before using.

2. Prepare molasses: In a saucepan, slowly reduce pomegranate juice to a syrupy consistency; let cool.

3. Slice tuna into 1/2-inch thick pieces and sear one side only in a hot nonstick skillet for 20 seconds. Cut seared tuna into a small dice and mix together with red pepper, poblano chile, virgin olive oil and lime juice. Season with salt and pepper to taste. Divide mixture and place in the centers of 6 plates. Surround tartare with drizzles of curry oil, molasses and crème fraîche.

4. In a bowl, toss endive with extra virgin olive oil and vinegar to coat. Season with salt and pepper. Place equal portions of dressed endive atop tartare; garnish with chive spears.

Southwest Crab Cakes with Ancho Chile Cream Sauce

Makes 4 Servings

    10 ounces lump crabmeat
    Southwest seasoning, commercial brands available at
        grocery stores
    2 ounces roasted corn kernels
    2 ounces mayonnaise
    2 ounces bread crumbs
    Clarified butter or canola oil for frying

Ancho Chile Cream Sauce:

    3 - 4 dried ancho chiles
    8 ounces heavily reduced chicken stock
    8 ounces heavy cream
    2 ounces white wine
    Salt to taste

1. Prepare sauce: Remove seeds and stems from ancho chiles. Cover with boiling water for 20 minutes. Remove from liquid (reserve liquid) and purée in a blender. If necessary, add a small amount of liquid to make a thick paste. Combine chicken stock, cream and white wine in heavy skillet or pot. Bring to a boil, reduce by 1/3. Add chile paste and simmer for 4 minutes.

2. Prepare crab cakes: Mix crabmeat, seasoning, corn and mayonnaise together very carefully to keep big chunks of crabmeat. Shape into 2 ounce patties; coat with bread crumbs and sauté in clarified butter until brown on both sides.

3. Divide sauce among 4 small plates. Place crab cakes on sauce on plates.

Eric Laqua

enjoys collecting rocks and minerals and says if he had not become a chef he would be designing and making jewelry. Born in Arzberg, Germany, Eric's extensive culinary experiences include many restaurants and hotels in Germany, Holland and Switzerland, even two years as officers' cook for the Holland-American Cruise Line.

Prior to being appointed The Phoenician's banquet chef in 1987, Eric's career as an executive chef included stopovers at The Sheraton Crescent Hotel, the Registry Resort and Phoenix Country Club, all in the Phoenix / Scottsdale area. He received the American Academy of Chefs title in 1974 and was designated a Certified Executive Chef in 1976. Also in 1976, he was selected "Chef of the Year" by the Phoenix Chefs Association. An American citizen since 1971, Eric is a member of the Academy of Chefs, the German Chefs Association, the International Chefs Association and the American Culinary Federation.

Eric Laqua — **The Phoenician** *— Scottsdale, Arizona*

Eddie Matney

Eddie Matney *is a natural born cook, but says he'd liked to have been an NBA basketball player. Admitting to being height challenged, he says he also loves the outdoors and "would love to be a fly fishing guide."*

Eddie's cooking career started in the Berkshires of Massachusetts, where he and partner Larry Cohn owned/operated the Stockbridge Cafe. In 1986 both moved to Arizona. Eddie opened Steamers; Larry ran the American Grill. Together they opened KousKous in 1988 and turned it into Eddie's Grill in 1990. The successful restaurant has received accolades from both the local and national media, including "Nation's Restaurant News" and "Food & Wine."

The effervescent Eddie hosts a weekly cooking segment on Fox10's morning news program and has been featured on the Television Food Network's "Ready, Set, Cook" program. He also participates in many charitable cooking events. When he's not in the restaurants' kitchens or on TV, Eddie loves to fly fish, ski, play basketball and work in his yard. He has a passion for warm cookies and milk and confesses he could eat a cheeseburger every day. When asked what people should know about him, Eddie says, "I'm very appreciative of what Phoenix has given to me."

Mo' Rockin' Shrimp

Makes 4 Servings

    12 large shrimp (16-20 per pound)
    1/4 cup onion, finely chopped
    5 garlic cloves, finely chopped
    1 shallot, finely chopped
    3 tablespoons butter
    3 tablespoons beer
    Dash of Worcestershire sauce

Chermoula Mix:

    1 cup olive oil
    1 cup lime juice
    1/2 cup Worcestershire sauce
    1/2 bunch cilantro, chopped
    1/2 bunch mint, chopped
    5 tablespoons ground coriander
    5 teaspoons crushed red pepper
    4 teaspoons ground black pepper
    4 teaspoons Dijon mustard
    3 teaspoons salt
    3 teaspoons cumin
    1 teaspoon cayenne pepper

1. Prepare the chermoula mix: Combine all ingredients in a mixing bowl. Mix well. Set aside.

2. Prepare the shrimp: Cook onion, garlic and shallot in 2 tablespoons butter until tender. Add shrimp and Worcestershire sauce; cook for 1 minute. Add beer; cook until liquid is reduced by half.

3. Add 1/4 cup chermoula mix (reserve remainder for another use). Swirl remaining cold butter into shrimp.

4. Pour into a serving bowl and serve hot.

Phyllo Wrapped Wild Mushroom Duxelles, Porcini Sauce

Makes 4 Servings
  Canola oil
  Salt and pepper to taste
  6 sheets phyllo dough
  1/4 cup melted butter
  Diced tomatoes for garnish

Wild Mushroom Duxelles:
  6 shallots, finely chopped
  8 garlic cloves, finely chopped
  1 pound button or cremini (Italian) mushrooms, chopped
  1 pound shiitake mushrooms, chopped
  1/2 pound chanterelle mushrooms, chopped
  8 cups veal stock (beef broth can be substituted)

Porcini Sauce:
  1/4 pound dried porcini mushrooms
  2 cups cream

1. Prepare the duxelles: Heat a large pan; add a little canola oil. Sweat the shallots and garlic in the pan until they begin to brown. Add the mushrooms; sweat in pan for a few minutes. Cover mushrooms with veal stock. Turn heat down and allow to simmer for 45 minutes. Strain the mushrooms and reserve the liquid for the sauce. Allow to cool.

2. Purée the mushrooms in a blender or food processor. Season the mixture with salt and pepper to taste.

3. Prepare the sauce: Add the dried porcini to the reserved liquid. Reduce the liquid over medium heat until the broth becomes thick. Add the cream. Reduce the mixture until it coats the back of a spoon. Season the sauce and strain through a fine colander. Purée porcinis; add to the duxelles mixture.

4. Prepare the phyllo wrapped duxelles: Lay one sheet of phyllo on a flat surface; brush lightly with melted butter. Top with another sheet. Repeat procedure with remaining sheets.

5. Heap the duxelles along the width of the phyllo dough about 1/4-inch from the edge. Slowly and carefully roll the dough, jellyroll fashion, over the duxelles. Place the roll on a sheet pan. Bake at 375 degrees until golden brown, 10 to 12 minutes. Remove from the oven and cut into eight pieces.

6. Assembly: Pour a little pool of sauce in the middle of the plate. Stand 2 phyllo rolls up in the center of each plate. Sprinkle the edge of the sauce with diced tomato.

Alan McLennan *began his culinary career as a cook at Masa's in the Vintage Court Hotel, San Francisco, working under renowned chef Masataka Kobayashi, whose cooking style uses Japanese aesthetics, California style and classical French techniques. He later traveled to Europe where he spent a few years cooking in luxury hotels throughout Europe and in London. The French press has described his work as "a marvelously creative interpretation of classic French cuisine."*

In 1992, Alan returned to the United States to become executive chef of Keswick Hall, a luxury resort outside of Charlottesville, Virginia, where "Town & Country" magazine later proclaimed, "Dinner is a ceremony to savor under Chef McLennan."

Alan returned to San Francisco in 1995 to become executive chef at the Cypress Club. His food is described as taking "traditional French cuisine to new heights by reinventing the classics with intense flavors and lively presentations."

Alan McLennan — **Cypress Club** *— San Francisco, California*

Louis

Osteen *is a South Carolina native for whom cooking at one time was only a hobby. "I had two hobbies," explains Louis, "one was cooking and one was taking pictures. I decided I would get a job doing one of those, whichever I got a job doing first. In a week's time, I was in the kitchen in a small French restaurant in Atlanta."*

Five years later, in 1980, he and his wife, Marlene, opened Pawleys Island Inn on Pawleys Island, South Carolina, where Louis became a leader in the exploding movement for indigenous American Cuisine. The Osteens moved to Charleston in 1989 and opened Louis's Charleston Grill at the Charleston Place Hotel. The restaurant was immediately praised by "Esquire" as one of the country's "Top 25 New Restaurants." Louis has been featured in many food publications, including "Food & Wine," "Gourmet," "Bon Appetit" and "Saveur," and on three occasions he has been recognized by the James Beard Foundation in their Distinguished Regional Chef series. Louis has appeared on the TV Food Network, CNN's "On the Menu" and is featured on the Discovery Channel's "Great Chefs of the South" series.

Wild Mushroom Ragout

Makes 4 Servings

 1/4 cup extra-virgin olive oil
 3/4 cup minced shallots
 1/4 cup minced garlic
 1/2 cup seeded, julienne poblano chile
 2 cups chicken stock
 1/2 cup dry white wine
 8 cups sliced wild mushrooms, cleaned and trimmed *
 2 tablespoons fresh thyme leaves, or a pinch of dried thyme
 1/8 teaspoon salt
 1/8 teaspoon freshly ground black pepper

1. Heat the olive oil over medium heat in a heavy stainless steel stock or soup pot. When the oil is hot, add the shallots, garlic and chile. Sauté on medium high heat for one minute; reduce heat to medium and continue to sauté for 5 to 7 minutes or until they are lightly brown, stirring frequently.

2. Heat chicken stock. Add wine and briskly simmer for 5 minutes to reduce the volume.

3. Add the mushrooms and thyme to the shallot mixture and continue to cook for 5 minutes, stirring often. Pour or spoon off any oil which may have come to the top. Add the hot chicken stock/wine mixture to the mushrooms and simmer for 8 to 10 minutes or until slightly thickened. It will still have a lot of juice. Stir in the salt and pepper.

4. Serve immediately or let the ragout cool to room temperature. Refrigerate covered for up to three days.

* The mushrooms may include morel, cèpes, trumpets, hedgehogs and shiitakes. Do not use portobello mushrooms as the black gills fall apart when the mushroom is sliced. Dried and reconstituted mushrooms may make up as much as 50% of the mix. After reconstituting dried mushrooms, strain liquid through a coffee filter; bring to a boil and reduce to a syrup. Add to dish.

Ecuadorian Shrimp Ceviche

Makes 4 Servings
  1 pound shrimp, peeled and cleaned
  1 large tomato, roasted, peeled and seeded
  2 jalapeño chiles, roasted, peeled and seeded
  2 red bell peppers, roasted, peeled and seeded
  1/2 medium onion, roasted
  3/4 cup fresh lime juice
  1/2 cup fresh orange juice
  1/4 cup tomato juice
  Tabasco®
  1 tablespoon sugar
  Salt

Garnish:

  1 small whole red onion sliced thin
  2 tablespoons chopped chives
  2 tablespoons chopped scallions
  Several whole cilantro leaves
  1 large tomato, chopped
  Popcorn
  Corn nuts

1. Place cleaned shrimp into a pot of boiling water for approximately 2 minutes (no longer); remove to an ice bath. Place all other ingredients in the blender and liquefy. Pour over the shrimp and chill.

2. Just before serving, toss garnishing ingredients, except the popcorn and corn nuts, into the ceviche. Place on individual serving plates, randomly sprinkling the popcorn and corn nuts around.

Douglas Rodriguez *was born in New York City to Cuban parents and moved to Miami in his early teens. After graduating from high school, he continued his cooking interests at Johnson & Wales University in Providence, Rhode Island. With culinary degree in hand, Douglas returned to South Florida to apply and hone his cooking skills. He subsequently set the Miami restaurant scene on fire. His "Nuevo Latino" cuisine found a home at Yuca Restaurant, where both received critical acclaim.*

Returning to New York, Douglas, now the "Manhattan Latin," has brought his "Nuevo Latino" cooking style to Patria. Open since February of 1994, Douglas and Patria have been the focus of food writers and various organizations. The James Beard Foundation awarded Douglas "1996 Rising Star Chef," recognizing him as the best chef in the nation age 30 or under. Besides his duties at Patria, he has a seemingly endless supply of energy. Douglas has produced a cooking video in Spanish and is currently at work on a dual language cookbook.

RoxSand

Scocos *was a painter and sculptor, but redirected her artistic energy to cooking eighteen years ago. She owned two restaurants and a catering business in Honolulu before returning to the mainland and opening RoxSand with husband Spyro Scocos in 1986.*

RoxSand has attended Madeleine Kamman's School for American Chefs and was nominated by the James Beard Foundation for America's Best Chef: Southwest (1995, 1996). She was inducted into the Scottsdale Culinary Hall of Fame in 1995 and is on the board of overseers for the Chefs Collaborative 2000. RoxSand is featured in "Food & Wine's America's Best Chefs," "Pastry Art & Design's The Art of the Plated Dessert," "Superchefs — Signature Recipes from America's New Royalty" (T. Wiley) and "Great Women Chefs" (Turner.)

RoxSand says her greatest accomplishments are her children, her "two blessings from heaven, Tatiana and Theo Isabella."

Very determined and serious about her career, she hopes young people beginning a cooking career will learn about ethics and principles and realize their position of helping to create an American heritage.

Blue Potato Strudel with Brown Butter Herb Sauce

Makes 6 Servings

    2 pounds Peruvian blue potatoes, peeled, cut into 1/8-inch slices (substitute Yukon Gold potatoes)
    6 tablespoons olive oil
    3/4 pound butter, divided use
    2 onions, chopped
    3/4 cup ricotta cheese
    3 tablespoons chopped flat leaf parsley
    3 tablespoons mixed chopped fresh herbs, such as chervil, tarragon, chives
    1 3/4 teaspoons salt, divided use
    Freshly ground black pepper
    2 eggs, beaten
    3 tablespoons chopped fresh chives
    12 sheets phyllo dough

1. In a large deep frying pan, heat oil over moderate heat. Add potatoes, 1 1/2 teaspoons salt, 3/4 teaspoon black pepper and cook, stirring frequently, until potatoes are tender and golden, about 20-25 minutes. Transfer to a large bowl.

2. In same pan, melt 4 tablespoons of butter over moderately low heat. Add onion, cook, stirring occasionally, until very soft, about 8 minutes. Add to potatoes and cool slightly.

3. In a food processor, pulse potato mixture in batches until coarsely chopped. Return to bowl; stir in eggs, ricotta, chives and parsley until just combined.

4. Melt 8 tablespoons butter in a saucepan. Lay one sheet of phyllo on work surface, short end towards you. Brush phyllo lightly with melted butter; top with another sheet. Place 1/2 cup of potato filling in bottom left corner. Shape into triangle, leaving a 1-inch margin on left side and along bottom. Fold right half of sheet onto the left; brush with butter. Turn up the bottom edge. Fold like flag, maintaining the triangular shape; brush once more with butter. Place the triangle, seam-side-down, on baking sheet. Repeat with remaining phyllo sheets and filling.

5. Heat oven to 350 degrees. Bake triangles until crisp and golden brown, about 15 minutes.

6. Melt remaining 12 tablespoons butter in large frying pan over moderate heat. Add remaining 1/4 teaspoon salt. Cook until butter turns golden brown, about 4 minutes. Remove from the heat and cool slightly. Stir in the herbs and pinch of pepper.

7. With a serrated knife, cut the triangles in half. Place one half in the center of a plate and lean other half against it, exposing filling. Drizzle butter sauce around each.

Sonoran Oyster Curry Stew

Makes 4 Servings

    1 teaspoon paprika
    1/4 teaspoon cayenne pepper
    1/2 teaspoon granulated garlic
    1/2 teaspoon granulated onion
    1 teaspoon sea salt (kosher salt can be substituted)
    1 teaspoon curry powder
    1/2 teaspoon dried thyme
    1/2 teaspoon cumin
    1/2 cup white wine
    2 cups clam broth
    4 cups heavy cream
    1 cup diced, grilled eggplant
    1 cup diced, grilled zucchini
    1 cup diced, grilled red onion
    1 cup diced, grilled tomato
    16 fresh Pacific oysters, shucked
    2 cups thinly sliced, washed and patted dry spinach

1. Combine paprika, cayenne, garlic, onion, salt, curry powder, thyme and cumin in a dry saucepan and toast over medium heat until fragrant. Stir in white wine.

2. Stir in clam broth and cream; increase heat to medium-high and continue cooking until mixture coats the back of a spoon. Add grilled vegetables and oysters; cook until heated through. Ladle into serving bowls; top with thinly sliced spinach.

Michael Shortino *is a third generation chef whose cooking career began at his family's Italian restaurant, Infantino's, in New York. He is a graduate of the Culinary Institute of America and among his many awards and honors is a nomination for "Top Chef in America Under 30" from the prestigious James Beard Foundation.*

"Cooking is all I've ever wanted to do," he says. "When you're cooking, you can get a unique sense of artistry, touching on virtually all the human senses — visual, taste, texture, aroma, even the sound when you describe a certain dish."

Michael is the corporate chef of Big 4 Restaurants, a Phoenix-based restaurant company, and is the executive chef/owner of the company's Steamers restaurant and a new catering operation entitled Events with Taste. He is known for his versatility as well as his flair with seafood.

"I love to cook just about everything," he says, "starting from scratch and using fresh ingredients, tapping into things that are available seasonally. I like to take a traditional Italian, French or another dish and put a new American flair to it, making it livelier, healthier."

California Chile
and Pasta Quiche

Ernst Springhorn,
a German native now a U.S. citizen, probably would have been a train engineer had he not been on track to becoming a chef. A certified executive chef and food service management professional, Ernst's culinary credentials include executive chef positions with Marriott Corporation, Four Seasons, Loewes Anatole and Sheraton. His culinary travels have taken him to Canada, Puerto Rico, Europe and many U.S. cities. He is a member of The American Culinary Federation and an officer in the Escoffier Society.

Gabriel's, located in the Viad building (formerly The Dial Corp), opened in 1991 with Ernst in command of its kitchen. The restaurant is a curious combination of setting and sustenance — American comfort food served in lavish surroundings. His culinary talents have taken the restaurant's signature dishes of meatloaf, chicken and dumplings, and pot roast to new heights.

When not at Gabriel's, Ernst can be found at a golf course. "I really, really, really like golf," he says. And when asked what people should know about him, Ernst credits his wife with many of his food ideas. "Sometimes I think too sophisticated or out-of-this world and she brings me down to earth. She's very, very supportive."

Makes 6 Servings

2 cups angel hair pasta, precooked al dente
1 1/2 cups roasted, peeled, julienne poblano peppers
1 cup sliced mushrooms
2 teaspoons finely chopped garlic
2 tablespoons chopped fresh cilantro
1/4 cup julienne celery
1/4 cup julienne carrots
1/4 cup julienne zucchini

Batter:

2 cups egg substitute
1/2 cup skim milk
1 cup grated skim mozzarella cheese
1/2 cup grated Parmesan cheese

1. Spray mini-bun or mini-muffin pan with non-stick spray. Combine batter ingredients, stir in remaining ingredients.

2. Pour batter into pans. Bake at 325 degrees in a water bath for approximately 15 to 20 minutes or until firm.

3. Serve with tomato concassé (cooked chopped tomatoes) seasoned with basil and Melba toast rounds, if desired.

Roasted Sea Scallops with Fennel, Mushrooms and Cranberry Beans

Makes 4 Servings

    8 heads baby fennel (substitute 2 heads fennel, cut into quarters)

    1 tablespoon extra-virgin olive oil

    Salt and freshly ground white pepper to taste

    4 medium fresh porcini or shiitake mushrooms or 1 portobello mushroom

    1 cup cranberry beans (available in specialty markets), cooked

    2 tablespoons chicken stock

    1/2 tablespoon lemon juice

    4 tablespoons Italian parsley leaves

    12 sea scallops (diver harvested preferred)

1. Preheat the oven to 375 degrees.

2. In a heavy, oven-proof skillet, heat 1/2 tablespoon olive oil over medium heat. Add fennel and cook until lightly browned. Season with salt and pepper and place in the oven for 10 minutes.

3. Cut the mushrooms into 1/4-inch slices and add to the skillet with the fennel; cook 10 more minutes. Remove pan from the oven, add cooked cranberry beans and place over medium heat. Add chicken stock and continue cooking until liquid is almost gone. Add lemon juice and remaining olive oil; season to taste. Add parsley leaves and set aside in a warm place.

3. Place a nonstick skillet over high heat. Season scallops with salt and pepper and add to the hot pan, searing on both sides until golden brown, about one minute per side.

4. Assembly: Divide the warm ragout of fennel, beans and mushrooms among four deep bowls. Place three scallops on top of each and serve immediately.

Alessandro Stratta's *family has been in the hotel and restaurant business for four generations, worldwide. Though Alessandro has a fantasy about a couple of fishing boats and Tahiti, cooking is his actual career of choice.*

His culinary talents are a blend of cultures and cuisines, having lived in Italy, France, Singapore, Pakistan and the United States. Prior to joining the Phoenician in 1989, Alessandro, a California Culinary Institute honors graduate, held cooking positions at Monte Carlo's The Louis XV at the Hotel de Paris, New York's Le Cirque restaurant and San Francisco's Stanford Court Hotel.

Alessandro was a James Beard Foundation nominee for America's Best Chef: Southwest and Best Hotel Chef in 1992, and in 1994, "Food & Wine" named him one of "America's Ten Best Chefs." When not in the resort's kitchens he likes to fish, travel and play guitar. He favors Indian food, "because it's hot and spicy and generally has good, hearty flavors," and sushi, "the freshness and lightness of it." And if he had to, he could pretty much live on chocolate, "really good chocolate."

Alessandro Stratta — **Mary Elaine's** *— Scottsdale, Arizona*

Cold Smoked Rock Shrimp
with Plum Tomato Relish

Makes 6 Servings

 4 ounces applewood chips
 1 1/2 pounds rock shrimp

Plum Tomato Relish:

 3 plum tomatoes, diced
 1 small white onion, chopped
 1/4 bunch cilantro, roughly chopped
 1 tablespoon tomato paste
 1 or 2 serrano chiles, diced or 2 to 3 shakes Tabasco® sauce

1. Prepare shrimp: Load a cold smoker with wood chips. Take a small baking tin and fill with ice. Place it above the wood chips and below the shrimp. Smoke the shrimp for 7 to 10 minutes. Remove shrimp and finish in a 350 degree oven for 10 minutes.

2. Prepare relish: Mix all the relish ingredients together.

3. Assembly: Make a ring of the plum tomato relish on the serving plate; arrange shrimp on the plum tomato relish.

Mark
Tarbell's *background is not limited to cooking alone. His knowledge of wines has many regarding him as being an authority. Mark's education includes earning a Grande Diplome d'Etudes Culinaires at Ecole de Cuisine la Varenne and studying at the Academie du Vin, both in Paris. Before returning to the United States, he worked in several renowned Paris eateries. He has taught food and wine classes at the Cambridge Wine Institute, the University of New Hampshire, Thunderbird School of International Management and the American Institute of Wine and Food. Prior to opening Tarbell's, Mark headed the food and wine programs at The Boulders resort, in Carefree, Arizona.*

Tarbell's has received accolades in such magazines as "Food & Wine," "Wine Spectator" and "Bon Appetit." Mark remains active in the Arizona Chapter of the American Institute Wine and Food and has conducted wine seminars and tastings throughout the Phoenix Valley.

Chimayo Chile Crusted Ahi Tuna with Soba Noodle Cucumber Salad and Cilantro Honey Vinaigrette

Makes 4 Servings
1/3 cup chimayo chile powder or ancho or pasilla powders
1/3 cup freshly ground cumin
1/3 cup freshly ground fennel seed
Salt
12 ounces center cut ahi tuna loin, must be block shaped
2 tablespoons canola oil

Cilantro Honey Vinaigrette:
2 small serrano chiles, stems removed
1 1/2 tablespoons honey
1/2 cup cilantro leaves
1 tablespoon mustard
3/4 cup canola oil
Salt and pepper to taste

Chile Oil:
2 tablespoons chile powder
3/4 teaspoon cumin
3/4 cup canola oil

Soba Noodle Cucumber Salad:
1 seedless cucumber, peeled and julienne cut
1/4 pound soba noodles, blanched and refreshed
2 tablespoons finely sliced scallions, green part only
1 box daikon radish sprouts

1. Combine chile powder, cumin and fennel. Lightly salt tuna and roll in spice mixture. Heat canola oil in a skillet over medium-high heat. Place tuna in pan and sear for only 10 seconds per side. Remove and refrigerate.

2. Prepare cilantro vinaigrette: In a blender, blend chiles, honey, cilantro and mustard until smooth. Slowly add oil.

3. Prepare chile oil: Heat chile powder and cumin together in a sauté pan until barely smoking; whisk in oil. When cooled, transfer to a glass jar and let stand overnight.

4. Prepare soba noodle salad:In a bowl, combine cucumber, noodles and scallions with Cilantro Honey Vinaigrette.

5. Mound equal portions of salad in the center of four plates. Cut ahi in thin slices; surround salad on each plate with ahi slices.

6. Drizzle chile oil on plate; garnish with daikon sprouts.

Ming Tsai

might have put his mechanical engineering degree from Yale to use had he not become a chef. "I've cooked all my life," says Ming. "My parents had a Chinese restaurant (in Dayton, Ohio) while I was growing up."

Ming studied at the Cordon Bleu in Paris and worked at Fauchon and Natacha. He achieved a master's in hotel administration and hospitality from Cornell University and worked several years in the hotel industry.

In 1992 Ming became sous chef at Silks at the Mandarin Hotel, San Francisco, and worked with Ken Hom. As an executive chef, he helped open Ginger Club, a tropical Asian restaurant in Palo Alto, and consulted in the restaurant business before arriving at Santacafé in June of 1995.

Ming has prepared a dinner at the James Beard House in New York, as well as hosting a James Beard Dinner at Santacafé with Drew Nieporent, chef/restaurateur, as emcee. Ming's easy going, yet informative teaching style has been well received by viewers of the TV Food Network's "Chef du Jour" series. He has also appeared on the network's "Ready, Set, Cook" show.

Bella Feldman ✦ *"War Toys"*

Installation Variable, Steel and Mixed Media   6" to 21" Height

Fritz Scholder ✦ *"Millennium #2"*

Oil on Canvas   80" x 68"

John Battenberg ✦ *"Mystic"*

Bronze   8' x 8'

John Edwards ✦ *"Dancing in the Heat"*

Oil on Canvas   36" x 48"

Jesús Bautista Moroles ✦ *"Granite Weaving"*

Fredericksburg granite   43 1/4" x 44" x 14"

Paul Sarkisian ✦ *"El Paso"*

Acrylic on Canvas   14' x 21'

Aung Aung Taik ✦ *"Batesian Mimicry"*
Oil on Canvas   63" x 83"

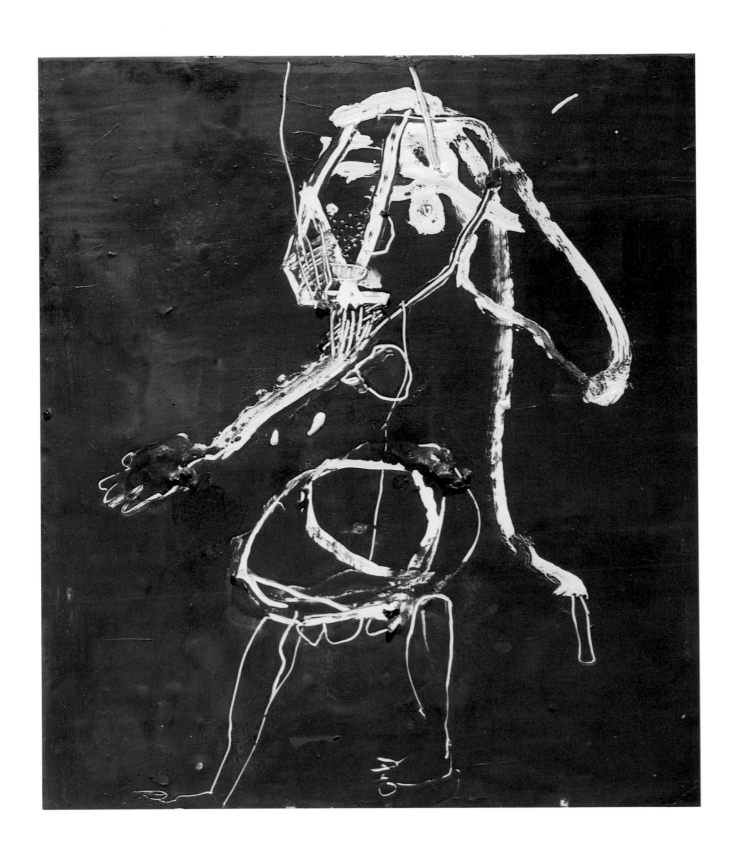

James Havard ✦ *"Swedish Blueprint"*
Oil and Wax on Board   16" x 14"

Beth Ames Swartz ✦ *"SHEN QI #3"*

Mixed Media with Gold Leaf on Canvas   20" x 24"

Mark Spencer ✦ *"Sphinx"*

Oil on Canvas   30" x 30"

Joel Coplin ✦ *"Red Room"*
Oil on Linen   72" x 64"

Masoud Yasami ✦ *"Composition with Arizona Sky"*

Acrylic and Oil on Canvas   48" x 60"

Otto Rigan ✦ *"Arc / Mark"*
Limestone and Glass   42" H x 64" W x 13" D

Michael Marlowe ✦ *"Kite"*

Oil on Canvas   98" x 72"

Merrill Mahaffey ✦ *"Curving Redwall"*
Acrylic on Canvas   32" x 48"

Buck McCain ✦ *"Generations"*

Oil on Canvas   40" x 60"

Philip C. Curtis ✦ *"The Viewers"*

Oil on Board   20.75" x 32"

ENTREES

Food styling -- Bobbi Jo & Razz Kamnitzer   *Photography -- Bob Carey*

Anton Brunbauer

Anton Brunbauer *is an Austrian native. He was born into a family of restaurateurs and innkeepers and began cooking as an apprentice at age 15. Had he not chosen a cooking career, he would have been involved with farming. Anton has worked in the finest hotels and restaurants in Austria, Switzerland, Germany, Liechtenstein and the United States. He is presently Regional Executive Chef of six Hyatt hotels and oversees the Scottsdale Hyatt's three dining options: the award-winning Golden Swan, the Squash Blossom and Ristorante Sandolo.*

Away from the Hyatt's kitchens, Anton can be found riding his Harley, skiing or, "what I probably enjoy most, watching my kids play soccer." He enjoys dining with his wife and is a fan of Japanese food. "It's something I don't make. It's light and you get a lot of different varieties and tastes."

Anton is recognized for his Southwestern influenced American cuisine. He was also instrumental in developing the Hyatt's Cuisine Naturelle, featuring flavorful menu items which meet American Heart Association guidelines. Cuisine Naturelle is offered at Hyatt hotels worldwide.

Honey Barbecued Salmon
on Baby Greens
with Cilantro Dressing

Makes 6 Servings

6 salmon fillets, 3 ounces each
Baby greens of choice (frisée, red oak, mâche, carrot leaves)

Honey Barbecue Sauce:

1 cup ketchup
1 cup honey
1/4 cup Pommery mustard
1/4 cup jalapeño peppers, chopped
1 ounce Japanese rice vinegar
1/2 ounce Tabasco® sauce
3 tablespoons brown sugar
1 tablespoon curry
1/2 tablespoon paprika
1 teaspoon soy sauce
1 teaspoon garlic, chopped
1 teaspoon vegetable oil
1/2 teaspoon Worcestershire sauce
1/2 teaspoon lemon juice
1/4 teaspoon ground pepper

Cilantro Dressing:

1/2 cup olive oil
1/8 cup malted vinegar
2 tablespoons chopped cilantro
1 tablespoon chopped shallots
1 teaspoon honey
Salt and pepper to taste

1. Prepare barbecue sauce: Mix all ingredients and chill.
2. Prepare cilantro dressing: Mix all ingredients and chill.
3. Prepare salmon: Dip salmon fillets in barbecue sauce and sauté or grill for approximately 3 minutes on each side.
4. Divide washed greens; place on plates. Top greens with salmon. Sprinkle with dressing.

Chicken in a Pot

Makes 4 Servings

    2 tablespoons olive oil
    1 whole kosher chicken, cut into pieces
    Kosher salt and pepper
    12 ounces beer
    3 carrots, peeled and cut into 2-inch pieces
    2 turnips, peeled and quartered
    3 to 4 small white onions, peeled
    1 cup chicken stock
    1 tablespoon chopped parsley
    4 ounces egg noodles, cooked according to package
       directions and buttered

1. Preheat oven to 400 degrees. Presoak a clay pot and lid for 20 minutes in cold water.
2. In a medium skillet, heat olive oil. Season chicken with salt and pepper and sear in the hot skillet. Remove chicken to presoaked clay pot. Deglaze skillet with beer and pour over chicken in pot. Add carrots, turnips, onions and chicken stock to clay pot.
3. Bake chicken in the clay pot, covered, in 400-degree oven for about 1 hour.
4. Remove from oven and season to taste with salt and pepper. Sprinkle with parsley. Serve chicken and vegetables in a bowl over buttered egg noodles. This dish is delicious served with matzoh balls instead of noodles.

James Cohen *loves Japanese food for its "simplicity and cleanliness." On those rare occasions when he's not in the resort's kitchens, he can be found biking, mushrooming and raising three children.*

About this recipe, he says, "just like my Bubby made." Bubby was his grandmother.

Read more about James on page 15.

Rigatoni Pomodoro

Michael DeMaria

had two college baseball scholarships, but chose to pursue cooking. Apprenticing at the Arizona Biltmore, he received classical training from the hotel's European chefs. After 11 years with the Westin Hotel Corporation, Michael moved to San Francisco to teach at the California Culinary Academy. His cooking career includes positions at San Francisco's Ritz-Carlton and the Wilshire Country Club in Los Angeles.

In 1992 Michael was one of 25 chefs comprising Team U.S.A. in the Culinary Olympics. The team and Michael received gold medals for their creations. He became executive chef of Lon's in 1995 and T. Cook's in early 1996. He has a passion for pasta, mashed potatoes and a dessert on T. Cook's menu, Bread Pudding with Amaretto Sauce. Though time off is a rare commodity, he manages now and then to squeeze in a round of golf. Says Michael about his profession, "I love to have fun in the kitchen. Cooking should be fun and shouldn't be made difficult. If you know the procedure and principles behind food, cooking is really only the art of adding and deleting."

In 1996, Michael's "The Royal Palms Cookbook," Sibling Press, made its debut, filled with recipe favorites from both Lon's and T. Cook's.

Makes 4 Servings

3/4 cup extra-virgin olive oil
8 Roma tomatoes, peeled, seeded, diced
1 tablespoon chopped shallots
2 tablespoons thinly sliced garlic
1 cup chicken stock or broth
1 tablespoon chopped parsley
2 tablespoons chopped basil
1 teaspoon salt
1/2 teaspoon black pepper
1 pound rigatoni, cooked al dente
1 tablespoon butter
Shaved Romano cheese

1. In a hot sauté pan, cook the olive oil, tomatoes, shallots and garlic over high heat for 3 minutes, reducing some of the excess liquid.
2. Add the chicken stock and reduce to 1/4 volume.
3. Add half of the herbs and all the salt and pepper.
4. Add hot pasta and butter to the tomato sauce; toss well.
5. Serve in individual bowls, sprinkled with remaining herbs and Romano cheese.

Chef's note: You can add extra vegetables to this dish to create a primavera-style pasta, or add prepared shrimp, fish or chicken to make this a heartier dish.

Whole Roasted Garlic-Studded Rack of Veal

Makes 4 Servings

 1 4 1/2-pound rack of veal
 6 to 8 garlic cloves, cut into eighths
 1/4 cup fresh rosemary leaves
 1/4 cup fresh thyme leaves
 1/4 cup fresh basil leaves
 Grated zest of 1 orange
 1 teaspoon kosher salt
 1/2 teaspoon black pepper
 1/4 cup olive oil

1. Place the veal on a platter and make holes all over it about an inch apart, by pushing a paring knife into the fat and turning it. Insert a garlic sliver into each hole.

2. Place the remaining garlic, rosemary, thyme, basil, orange zest, salt and pepper in a food processor fitted with a steel blade and pulse until finely chopped. Add the olive oil and process until the mixture forms a chunky paste.

3. Rub the mixture all over the veal. Cover and refrigerate for at least 2 hours, or overnight.

4. Preheat the oven to 425 degrees or prepare the grill.

5. Roast or grill the veal, uncovered, for about 25 minutes. Let the meat rest for 15 to 20 minutes. Carve one bone per person.

Todd English

has been bestowed with many awards and recognitions, including 1991 Rising Star Chef and 1994 America's Best Chef: Northeast by the James Beard Foundation.

About this recipe he says, "Serve this impressive dish for a truly elegant occasion when you're not concerned about your budget. Roasting the whole rack is the most succulent and delicious way to serve veal."

Read more about Todd on page 17.

Christopher
Gross
happened into the restaurant business out of financial necessity: At age 12, he wanted a dirt bike for which his mother told him to earn the money. He did. Years and a few restaurants later, Christopher has earned respect as a celebrated chef. His cooking highlights include positions at Chez Albert in Paris; L'Orangerie and Century Plaza Hotel in Los Angeles; and La Champagne and Le Relais in Scottsdale.

In 1990, Christopher opened Christopher's and Christopher's Bistro. The restaurants have received laudatory ink in "Food & Wine," "Conde Nast Traveler" and "The New York Times." Christopher has been honored in "Food & Wine" as one of "America's Ten Best New Chefs" and in 1995 the James Beard Foundation awarded him America's Best Chef: Southwest. Christopher is not likely to pass up chocolate, foie gras or, when time permits, a motorcycle ride.

White Fish
in Fennel Broth

Makes 4 Servings
   8 fennel bulbs
   1 cup julienne carrot
   1 cup julienne turnip
   1 cup julienne celery
   Salt and pepper to taste
   4 fillets of sea bass (4 ounces each)

1. Juice fennel bulbs and place liquid in a saucepan. Over high heat, reduce liquid by half.

2. Meanwhile blanch vegetables in boiling water; transfer to ice water, drain and set aside.

3. Place fennel broth (approximately 2 cups) in a sauté pan and bring to a simmer. Lightly season fillets with salt and pepper and place in broth. Poach fillets in broth until done. Transfer fillets to shallow serving bowls; garnish each with equal portions of blanched vegetables. Pour remaining broth around fillets in the bowls.

Grilled Veal Loin
with Fried Shallots
and Chipotle Pasta

Makes 2 Servings

4 (3-ounce) slices veal loin
4 tablespoons olive oil
2 tablespoons chopped shallots
Salt and pepper to taste
Chopped cilantro for garnish

Chipotle Pasta:

1 cup all-purpose flour
1 tablespoon chipotle chile purée
1 extra-large egg
1 teaspoon olive oil
Salt and pepper to taste
Butter to taste

1. Prepare pasta: Mix flour with chipotle purée in food processor. Add egg; mix. Add olive oil and salt. Process until mixture forms a small ball around the blade. It may be necessary to add 1 teaspoon water.

2. Pass dough through pasta machine to desired size.

3. Cook pasta in boiling, salted water for approximately 1 minute or until al dente. Drain. Add salt, pepper and butter to taste.

4. Brush veal loin with a little of the olive oil and grill over high heat for 3 minutes on each side.

5. Place remaining olive oil in a frying pan over high heat; add shallots and stir-fry until brown.

6. Divide pasta among 2 serving plates. Top with veal; garnish with fried shallots and chopped cilantro.

Vincent Guerithault, *a native of France, is the chef/owner of Vincent Guerithault on Camelback. He has received national acclaim for his expertise in combining classic French cookery with ingredients indigenous to the American Southwest. Had he not embarked on a cooking career Vincent says, "I would have loved to travel and just be a travel agent. We've been traveling a lot and I think it's a lot of fun."*

After his culinary training in France and apprenticing at Maxim's in Paris, Vincent became Jean Banchet's sous chef at the renowned Le Francais in Wheeling, Illinois. He moved to Arizona in 1980 and opened Vincent Guerithault on Camelback in January, 1986. The restaurant has been featured in "Food & Wine," "Gourmet" and "Bon Appetit," to name a few, and has received numerous awards. In January 1996, Mobil Travel Guide awarded the restaurant a Four-Star rating.

In 1994, Ten Speed Press published "Vincent's Cookbook", written by Vincent with Esquire's food and wine critic, John Mariani. The book features his favorite foods with the exception of a particular confection. Seems Vincent is smitten by chocolate Dove Bars, and confesses, "The freezer is always full of Dove Bars."

Gerald Hirigoyen

was born in the Basque region of France. He knew from the early age of 13 that he wanted to be a chef. After studying and practicing the art of pastry making, he moved to Paris and apprenticed for master pâtissiers, Jean Millet and Dennis Ruffel.

Gerald emigrated to the U.S. and San Francisco in 1980. His culinary addresses include Le Castel in Pacific Heights; Lafayette, a downtown bistro; and Le St. Tropez as executive chef. In 1991 he opened Fringale. The menu is inspired by his Basque background, with straightforward, bright flavors.

In 1994 he was named one of "Food & Wine's Ten Best New Chefs in America." He has authored a cookbook, "Bistro" (Sunset Books), and is currently working on another book with his wife, Cameron, to be published by HarperCollins.

In February of 1996 Gerald, with partner J.B. Lorda, opened a second restaurant, Pastis, which serves French-American fusion fare in a brasserie atmosphere.

Crispy Striped Bass with Cucumber and Lemon-Coriander Vinaigrette

Makes 4 Servings

4 medium size cucumbers, peeled
2 teaspoons salt
2 teaspoons coriander seeds
1/8 cup + 2 tablespoons fresh squeezed lemon juice
1/8 cup water
1/4 cup chopped roasted bell peppers
1/3 cup + 1/4 cup + 1 tablespoon olive oil
1/2 teaspoon white pepper
1/8 cup fresh chopped chives
1/8 cup fresh chopped parsley
4 fillets of striped bass (about 5 ounces each)

1. Using a mandoline, julienne the cucumbers in lengthwise "spaghetti-like" strips, stopping at the seeded core. Place cucumber in a bowl, sprinkle with 1 teaspoon salt, mix together and set aside, about 20 minutes, to remove excess water from cucumbers

2. Meanwhile, combine coriander seeds, 2 tablespoons fresh lemon juice, water, roasted bell peppers, 1/3 cup olive oil, 1 teaspoon salt and white pepper in a blender; mix at high speed for 1 minute or until ingredients are smooth and creamy. Strain the sauce through a sieve to remove any coarse ingredients and set aside.

3. Rinse cucumber with clear water to remove salt. In a warm sauté pan, place 1/4 cup olive oil, 1/8 cup lemon juice, cucumber, salt and pepper to taste, and sauté until warmed through. Add the chives and parsley, mix together well; keep warm.

4. In a medium sized sauté pan, warm 1 tablespoon olive oil over medium high heat. Score the skin sides of the fillets before placing them (skin-side-down) in the sauté pan. Sauté 3 to 5 minutes on each side. Lightly strain the cucumber; arrange equal portions in a circular fashion in the center of four plates. Place fillets on top of the cucumber and spoon the vinaigrette around the circular edge of the plates.

Hannah's Roasted Chicken

Makes 4 Servings

   2 roasting chickens, 3 to 4 pounds each, split

Adobo Marinade:
   1 cup roasted whole garlic cloves
   1/2 7-ounce can chipotle peppers in adobo sauce
   1 cup soy sauce
   1 tablespoon black pepper
   1/2 cup olive oil

1. Prepare marinade: Into a blender, place garlic cloves, chipotle peppers and sauce, soy sauce and black pepper. Blend on high speed until puréed. With blender running, slowly pour in the oil; blend until emulsified. Hold at room temperature if using immediately or refrigerate, covered, for use later. Bring to room temperature before using.

2. Prepare the chicken: Heat the oven to 350 degrees. Remove excess fat and skin from chickens and toss the chicken pieces with 1 1/2 cups of the marinade (reserve remainder).

3. Place chicken, cut side down, on sheet pans or rimmed baking sheets. Roast, uncovered, for 35 to 45 minutes, until juices run clear and chicken is crisp. Serve with mashed potatoes and fresh vegetables if desired. Pass the remainder of the sauce separately.

Tudie Johnson *says, "I don't know what else I'd do if I was not a chef. I was in real estate, managed properties and buildings. I grew up on a ranch... rodeoed, farmed and all that kind of stuff. But I don't think I'd do that again."*

Tudie's cooking career began out of necessity at the Turtle Cove restaurant in Port Arkansas, Texas. "Basically I needed a job. I washed dishes, bussed tables, cooked." She stayed at the restaurant for seven years before joining Sam's Cafe, in Dallas. Tudie moved to Phoenix to open the Arizona Center's Sam's Cafe and presently oversees Sam's in the Biltmore Fashion Park and the new Sam's in Scottsdale. She's a spicy food fan and loves chocolate, especially Sam's chocolate truffle cake. When not in the kitchen she enjoys gardening and building Southwestern-style furniture with her husband.

Tudie is an enthusiastic supporter of many Phoenix-area culinary events and has been recognized nationally for her work with Share Our Strength's annual Taste of the Nation, a nationwide benefit for hunger relief.

Razz Kamnitzer,

a Venezuelan native and seventh generation chef of German descent, almost became a veterinarian. "I tried it for two years," says the over-energetic Razz, "then, I couldn't afford it."

Razz received his formal culinary training at the National Hotel School of Lausanne in Switzerland and the Culinary Institute of America. His career includes positions at New York's Escoffier Room and Boston's Sheraton Hotel. Razz has owned and operated several restaurants in the Phoenix area and cooked at The Registry Resort and the Pointe Hilton Resort at Tapatio Cliffs. He opened Razz's Restaurant and Bar in the fall of 1995.

Razz is recognized for his inventive cuisine incorporating edible flowers and fresh herbs and vegetables, many of which are grown in his "growing" chef's garden. If asked about a favorite food, he does not hesitate, "Veal sweetbreads. It's my favorite food of all times. I mean of all times."

Razz's enthusiasm for cooking is nonstop. In addition to teaching cooking classes and cooking on local TV, Razz has cooked at the James Beard House and has been featured on the Television Food Network's "Chef du Jour" and "Ready, Set, Cook" programs. "Esquire" magazine selected Razz's Restaurant as one of the nation's best new restaurants in 1996.

Spiced Cashew and Mustard Seed Crusted Tuna with Watermelon Salsa

Makes 4 Servings

- 20 ounces ahi tuna cut into four 5-ounce portions
- 1/4 cup all-purpose flour
- 2 eggs, beaten
- 1/2 cup ground cashew nuts
- 1/2 cup mustard seed
- 1/2 cup olive oil for frying
- 1/2 cup bread crumbs

Seasoning Spice:

Combine equal amounts of the following to make 1/4 cup: coriander, curry, cumin, thyme, sage, chile powder, ginger, rosemary, paprika, cayenne pepper, garlic powder, celery seed, dry mustard, salt and pepper.

Watermelon Salsa:

- 2 cups peeled, seeded and diced watermelon
- 1 tablespoon sliced onions
- 1/2 cup sliced peppers — poblano, jalapeño, red bell
- 1 teaspoon chopped garlic
- 3 tablespoons chopped cilantro
- Juice of two limes
- Salt and pepper to taste

1. Prepare the salsa: In a mixing bowl, combine all ingredients and season with salt and pepper.

2. Prepare the tuna: Combine the ground nuts, mustard seed and bread crumbs and set aside. On a plate, combine the seasoning mix with the flour; roll the tuna pieces in it. After rolling in the mixture, dip into beaten eggs, allowing the excess to drip off; roll again in cashew-mustard seed-crumb mix. Pan fry in hot olive oil until golden in color. Top with Watermelon Salsa.

Salmon Steak on Mashed Potatoes with Saffron Broth

Makes 4 Servings

1 pound baking potatoes, such as russets
1/2 cup milk
2 tablespoons unsalted butter, divided use
4 fresh skinless salmon steaks, 6 to 7 ounces each, 1 inch thick
1/2 tablespoon olive oil
2 tablespoons finely minced shallots
1 sprig thyme, finely minced
1/3 cup dry white wine
1 small dessert apple
1 pinch saffron threads
1/2 tablespoon cream
1 tablespoon chives, finely sliced
1 tomato, peeled, seeded and diced
Salt and freshly ground pepper

1. Preheat the oven at 325 degrees.

2. Scrub the potatoes, prick with a fork and cook (skin-on) in a pot, covered by 1 inch of salted water. Simmer gently until tender (20 to 30 minutes). Drain; as soon as potatoes can be handled, remove skins. Mash or pass potatoes through a food mill. Bring milk to a boil; gradually whisk into potatoes. Add 1 1/2 tablespoons butter little by little, and continue whisking until potatoes are fluffy and light. Season to taste. If the mashed potatoes seem to be a bit firm, stir in additional hot milk. Keep hot.

3. Prepare salmon: Sprinkle salmon steaks with salt and freshly ground pepper on both sides. Brush the bottom of a casserole dish with 1/2 tablespoon olive oil. Sprinkle with minced shallots and thyme. Place salmon steaks in the dish. Add the white wine and 5 to 6 tablespoons of water. Cover with a sheet of aluminum foil and place in a 325 degree oven for about 12 to 15 minutes.

4. Peel, halve and core apple. Cut it into small cubes. Sauté the cubes briefly in remaining 1/2 tablespoon butter until tender (2 to 3 minutes). Set aside.

5. When salmon steaks are done (to be perfectly cooked, the salmon steaks should be slightly rare in the middle and moist), transfer the cooking broth into a small sauce pot. Add the saffron threads and 1/2 tablespoon cream; simmer for 2 minutes. Add the chives, cooked apple and the tomato. Stir gently with a spoon and adjust seasoning with salt and pepper.

6. Spoon mashed potatoes in the center of serving plates. Carefully place salmon steaks on top of potatoes. Spoon the saffron broth around.

Hubert Keller

says if he were not a chef, he'd be a drummer in a rock and roll band. Seems he often sat in with his brother's small band. "I did pretty good, I got a kick out of it," says the French-born Keller. "Or driving a race car. I love speed."

Hubert trained with Paul Bocuse at Collonges, near Lyon, France. His culinary career includes positions at several restaurants in France, even work on a cruise liner. Before his arrival in San Francisco, he spent two years at Roger Verge's La Cuisine du Soleil, in Sao Paulo, Brazil. In 1986, Hubert became co-owner of Fleur de Lys with Maurice Rouas. Since its opening, the restaurant and Hubert have garnered many prestigious awards and recognitions.

Hubert loves desserts, especially pastries and ice cream. "If the doctor told me no more meat or seafood and that I had to live on desserts, I would say, 'Great!'" When not at Fleur de Lys, he can be found riding his motorcycle or scuba diving. Hubert has also written a cookbook: "The Cuisine of Hubert Keller," published by Ten Speed Press.

George Mahaffey

went to graduate school to study philosophy and mathematical logic. He decided to cook instead. "I think basically I like doing things with my hands and I like working on projects. There's a lot of lore and philosophy and science in cooking. It's a natural thing for me."

George's cooking positions include the Hotel Hershey in Hershey, Pennsylvania; The Cloister Hotel on Sea Island, Georgia; and prior to joining The Little Nell as executive chef in 1992, he was executive chef of The Hotel Bel-Air in Los Angeles.

At The Little Nell, George broadened his approach to cooking. His award-winning American Alpine Cooking utilizes products from the Colorado Rocky Mountains and is often influenced by the flavors of the Mediterranean, Asia and Central America. When not in the kitchen, he enjoys music — especially the blues — and is something of a car nut. "If there is any true hobby that I have, it's messing around with my [five] kids." George eats just about anything and says, "it just doesn't get any better than a fresh apple pie." And on being a chef, "I'm kind of like a Virginia country boy that got lucky and got a good job."

Dijon and Bread Crumb Coated Trout with Mild Garlic Mashed Potatoes and Lemon Sage Jus

Makes 6 Servings

6 red trout fillets (8-ounces each), halved
Salt and pepper
Dijon mustard
Canola oil for frying
3/4 cup sliced white mushrooms
3/4 cup chopped red and gold tomatoes
1/3 cup thinly sliced on the bias scallions
2 cups chicken broth
4 tablespoons fresh lemon juice
3/4 cup whole butter, softened
2 tablespoons chopped sage

Herb Bread Crumbs:
5 cups fresh white bread crumbs
1 cup parsley, chopped
1/2 cup basil leaves, chopped
1/3 cup chives, chopped

Garlic Cream:
1 1/2 cups cream
2 tablespoons chopped garlic
1/4 cup whole butter
1/4 teaspoon nutmeg

Garlic Mashed Potatoes:
1 quart red new potatoes, cooked
1 1/2 cups garlic cream (recipe)
Salt & pepper

1. Prepare herb bread crumbs: Combine all ingredients and process in a food processor until evenly blended and a light green color develops. Set aside.

2. Prepare garlic cream: Combine all ingredients in a saucepan and bring to a boil. Remove and keep warm.

3. Prepare garlic mashed potatoes: Place potatoes in a mixer and beat until smooth. Add cream and seasonings; blend together well. Remove and keep warm.

(Continued on next page)

(Continued from previous page)

4. Prepare the trout: Season the trout fillets with salt and pepper. Brush flesh-side only with mustard; press mustard-coated sides of fish into the herb bread crumbs. Cook flesh-side-down on a griddle or in a nonstick pan with a little canola oil for approximately 3 minutes on each side.

5. Meanwhile, heat a small amount of oil in a sauté pan over high heat. Add mushrooms; sauté for 1 minute. Add scallion, tomatoes, chicken broth and lemon juice. Add butter and sage; cook until slightly thickened, about 2 minutes.

6. Place about 3/4 cup mashed potatoes in the center of six serving plates. Ladle equal amounts of mushroom sauce around potatoes. Top potatoes with trout fillets.

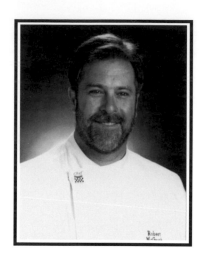

Robert
McGrath *started cooking at a young age and didn't change careers, though he once had an interest in genetics and biochemistry. Then, there are times, "when I just want to sit on a beach in Costa Rica and crack coconuts. That's usually around budget time."*

Robert received his formal culinary training at the Cordon Bleu, in Paris, and at the Culinary Institute of America. He has traveled through the Caribbean and Europe and held cooking positions in Florida, California, New York and Texas. Prior to becoming chef de cuisine at Windows on the Green, Robert had been chef/owner of Sierra restaurant in Houston. His cooking has been recognized with many awards including "Food & Wine's America's Ten Best New Chefs," in 1989, and the 1994 Evian Healthy Menu Award, a competition co-sponsored by "Gourmet." Robert also has received nominations in 1994 and 1995 from the James Beard Foundation for America's Best Chef: Southwest.

Robert likes Japanese or Thai food or a simple roasted chicken. Away from the resort's kitchen, he enjoys horseback riding, fly fishing and hiking. His food philosophy: "Having fun is the whole key to everything. If you're enjoying yourself, it definitely translates out to the dining room."

Roasted Rack of Lamb, Chilled Sweet Potatoes, Red Chile Adobo, Grilled Papaya Salsa

Makes 4 Servings

4 lamb racks, 9 ounces each
Kosher salt and freshly cracked pepper to taste

Chilled Sweet Potatoes:
2 cups peeled sweet potatoes, cut into 1/2-inch dice
1 tablespoon chopped onion
2 tablespoons butter
1 tablespoon sour cream
1 tablespoon crushed cascabel chile
1 tablespoon roasted, peeled and diced poblano chile
1 teaspoon finely chopped fresh epazote, or 1/2
    teaspoon dried
1 teaspoon finely chopped garlic
Salt and pepper to taste

Grilled Papaya Salsa:
1/2 papaya, peeled and seeded
1 tablespoon diced red pepper
1 tablespoon finely chopped red onion
1 tablespoon finely chopped jalapeño
1 tablespoon chopped cilantro
1 tablespoon fresh lime juice

Red Chile Adobo Sauce:
1 tablespoon olive oil
1/2 cup diced tomatoes
1 tablespoon finely chopped onion
1 teaspoon crushed ancho chile
1 teaspoon crushed guajillo chile (substitute dried red chile)
1/2 cup chicken stock
1 tablespoon red wine vinegar
1 teaspoon sugar
1/2 teaspoon achiote paste (available at Latin markets)
1/2 teaspoon pickling spice

Salad:
20 asparagus spears
1 cup curly endive, washed and torn into bite-sized pieces
1/2 cup coarsely chopped, oil-packed, sun-dried tomatoes
1 tablespoon olive oil (or oil from the sun-dried tomatoes)

(Continued on next page)

(Continued from previous page)

1. Prepare the potatoes: Place potatoes and onion in a shallow, heavy pan and roast in a preheated 400-degree oven until brown, about 15 to 20 minutes. In a medium bowl, mix the butter, sour cream, chiles, epazote and garlic. Add potatoes and onion and mix well; season with salt and pepper; cover and chill.

2. Prepare the salsa: On a hot barbecue or grill, place the papaya, flesh-side-down, and grill until lightly browned. Remove from heat and cut into 1/4-inch dice. Measure 1/2 cup of papaya (save remainder for another use) and put into a medium bowl. Add red pepper, red onion, jalapeño, cilantro and lime juice. Set aside in a cool place.

3. Prepare the sauce: In a heavy skillet heat the olive oil over medium heat and sauté the tomatoes, onions and chiles until onions are soft, about 3 minutes. Add the remaining ingredients. Bring to a boil and reduce by 1/3 (until about 2/3 cup remains). Place mixture in a blender, purée and strain. Set aside.

4. Prepare the salad: Blanch the asparagus in boiling, salted water for 3 to 5 minutes or until barely cooked. Plunge spears into ice water to stop the cooking; drain. In a large bowl, toss asparagus with curly endive, sun-dried tomatoes and olive oil. Add salt to taste.

5. Prepare the lamb: Season the lamb racks with salt and pepper and grill over a hot barbecue or grill until cooked to the desired doneness, about 5 minutes per side for medium rare. Remove all bones except the end bone, if desired, or serve with the bones intact.

6. Assembly: On each of four plates, place the chilled sweet potatoes off center, toward the upper right. If using boned lamb, slice each rack on a bias into approximately 5 slices and layer the slices around the potatoes. If leaving the bones on, slice the racks into individual chops and arrange around the potatoes. Drizzle the sauce over the lamb and potatoes. Place salad on the bottom right of the plate and place a tablespoon of the salsa on top of the lamb.

Roland Oberholzer

began his cooking career as a teen in an apprentice program at the Hotel Linde, in his native Switzerland. He honed his skills at various Swiss hotels and restaurants including the Grand Hotel Kronenhof, Ochsen Hotel and Wirtschaft Zum Doktorhaus, a restaurant and convention center.

Roland moved to Canada in 1982, where he was a private chef. He became a sous chef at Rosedale Oyster, in Toronto, in 1985 and chef of Vagara Bistro in Toronto in 1986. When the owners of Vagara Bistro opened a second restaurant in Scottsdale, Arizona, in the late 1980s, Roland was asked to head its kitchens. He did, and after a few successful years, he ventured into restaurant ownership with the opening of Roland's in 1994. It's the perfect showcase for his innovative, updated continental cuisine.

Fillet of Red Snapper
with Champagne Sauce

Makes 4 Servings

4 snapper fillets, 6 ounces each
2 cups champagne
1 tablespoon chopped onions
1 tablespoon unsalted butter
1/2 cup heavy cream
Salt and pepper
Lemon juice
Worcestershire sauce
1 teaspoon chopped parsley
1/2 teaspoon chopped fresh tarragon
1/2 teaspoon finely diced red pepper

1. Preheat oven to 400 degrees. Butter a large rectangular dish, big enough to hold the fillets; spread onions evenly on bottom of dish. Season the snapper fillets on both sides with salt, pepper, lemon juice and Worcestershire sauce. Place fillets on top of the onions; pour champagne over and cover with aluminum foil. Bake for about 5 minutes or until done.

3. Remove fillets from baking dish and place on a warm serving platter. Keep warm. Add cream to the pan; reduce the sauce until thick and creamy. Add herbs and red pepper; mix well.

Chicken & Dumplings

Makes 4 Servings

    32 ounces chicken stock
    12 ounces carrots, cubed
    12 ounces celery, cubed
    12 ounces onion, cubed
    1 pound chicken tenders
    4 tablespoons cornstarch, to thicken

Dumplings:
    4 cups flour
    1 1/2 teaspoons baking powder
    3 eggs
    3/4 cup buttermilk

1. Prepare dumplings: Combine all dry ingredients. Add egg and milk and mix to a smooth consistency (noodle-like dough).

2. Roll out to 1/8-inch thickness. Cut into 1 by 2 1/2-inch strips (4 dumplings = 1 serving). Remaining dumpling dough may be refrigerated for up to a week or frozen until ready to use.

3. Assembly: Cook vegetables simultaneously with the dumplings (16 strips) in chicken stock for 10 to 12 minutes. Add chicken tenders. Simmer for another 5 minutes or until desired consistency is obtained. Season to taste. Thicken stock with cornstarch, if needed. Serve in individual crocks or family-style bowls.

Ernst Springhorn *is known for his American comfort food cooking at Gabriel's. However, he does admit a love of "all that European sausage and bread stuff, any kind of sausage and a different variety of breads."*

Chicken and dumplings and another American comfort classic, meatloaf, have been menu mainstays at Gabriel's since its debut in 1991. Recently, still another timeless dish, pot roast, was added to Gabriel's entree repertoire.

Read more about Ernst on page 28.

Ernst Springhorn — **Gabriel's** *— Phoenix, Arizona*

Scott Tompkins

Scott Tompkins *cooked and studied accounting in school, but says, "I figured out in college that accounting was boring and stuck with cooking."*

Scott's cooking style reflects his fascination with history, especially the history of Oriental cuisine. The former executive chef of the Arizona Club — a position he held for nine years — Scott is recognized for his Asian-influenced food. He is presently wowing diners at Marco Polo, a quaint cafe known for its inventive fusion of Italian and Oriental flavors.

Scott is a self-described "car freak." He likes restoring cars and is the proud owner of a 1938 Ford Coupe. He is adamant about preserving the small farms of the nation and is actively involved with many charities including the Liver Alliance, American Heart Institute and the Cystic Fibrosis Auxiliary and Kids' Camp. Each year for the past eleven years, he and other chefs have donated their cooking talents and time to the camp. Scott is a member of the American Culinary Federation, Arizona Restaurant Association board member and Scottsdale Culinary Institute board advisor.

Osso Buco Gremolata Veal Shanks

Makes 2 Servings

All-purpose flour for dredging
2 veal shanks, approximately 1-inch thick
2 tablespoons vegetable oil
2 carrots, diced
1 stalk celery, diced
1/2 small onion, diced
4 cloves garlic
2 tomatoes, peeled, seeded and diced
2 cups white wine
2 cups veal stock or beef broth
Fresh basil
Black pepper
2 tablespoons tomato paste

Gremolata:

1 clove garlic, minced
1 tablespoon minced Italian parsley
1 tablespoon minced lemon rind

1. Dredge shanks in flour, shaking off excess. Set aside.

2. In a skillet, heat oil over medium heat. Add shanks and brown on both sides. Deglaze with wine. Add stock, vegetables, basil, pepper and tomato paste. Reduce heat, cover and simmer for 2 hours or until meat almost falls from the bone.

3. Prepare gremolata: Combine all ingredients in a small bowl.

4. Remove veal shanks to serving platter or individual plates; sprinkle with gremolata. Serve with pasta or rice, spooning vegetables and sauce over top, if desired.

Seared Beef Fillet with Basil Salad and Tomato Gorgonzola Salsa

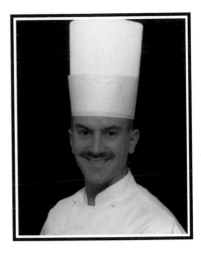

Makes 2 Servings

  2 medium tomatoes, diced
  1 small red onion, finely diced
  1 yellow banana pepper, finely diced
  1/2 sweet yellow pepper, finely diced
  3 tablespoons crumbled Gorgonzola
  1 tablespoon chopped fresh oregano
  Juice and zest of 1 lemon
  Salt and freshly ground black pepper, divided use
  Canola or vegetable oil to sear
  4 beef fillets, 2 ounces each
  20 basil leaves
  Olive oil
  Aged balsamic vinegar

1. Prepare the salsa: Combine tomatoes, onion, peppers, Gorgonzola, oregano, lemon. Salt and pepper to taste; set aside.

2. Heat oil in a heavy skillet to the smoke point. Salt and pepper the fillets, and sear to medium rare.

3. Just prior to serving, toss the basil leaves with a little olive oil and balsamic vinegar, just enough to moisten. Season with salt and pepper.

4. Place salad on 2 serving plates; top each with a fillet and salsa.

Scott Uehlein *graduated from the Culinary Institute of America in 1985 and has a growing fascination with vineyards. It's not surprising since he credits his mentor, Madeleine Kamman of the School for American Chefs at Beringer Vineyards in California, with being the most influential person in his career. Scott's culinary style has been further shaped by the cooking positions he's held at restaurants in Washington, DC, Virginia, Philadelphia and New York. He credits his culinary success with his ability to work with indigenous ingredients.*

Scott has received laudatory ink in "Esquire" in 1992 as one of the "Top Ten Rising Stars" and was featured in a July, 1996, "Bon Appetit" article. He has been honored by the James Beard Foundation as one of the Best Resort Chefs of America, as well as a winner in the Scottsdale Culinary Festival's Mayor's Culinary Cup in 1995 and 1996.

Janos

Wilder *cooked throughout high school and college initially as a means of support while attaining a political science degree. After graduation he continued to cook, gaining expertise at such restaurants as Le Mirage, a French restaurant in Santa Fe, New Mexico and La Reserve and Le Duberne, both in Bordeaux, France, where he continued to learn the techniques of classical and nouvelle cuisines.*

Janos and his wife, Rebecca, opened their restaurant, Janos, in 1982, in a National Historic Landmark home on the grounds of the Tucson Museum of Art. The restaurant quickly gained local and national acclaim for its inspired cooking style blending French techniques with ingredients Janos obtained from local growers. In 1990, Janos was named "Rising Star of American Cuisine" by the James Beard Foundation, and has been nominated by the Foundation as "America's Best Chef: Southwest" the past four years. He likes the gutsy flavors of Thai food and loves coffee ice cream. Spare time — "What's that?" he asks, is reserved for his family. If he wasn't cooking today, Janos says he'd be involved with, "some sort of public service work... or basketball if there was any market for a 5'6" slow, white point guard with a spotty outside shot and no leaping ability."

Lobster with Papaya, Champagne Sauce and Spinach Carrot Timbales

Makes 4 Servings

   3 cups dry champagne
   2 tablespoons honey
   2 tablespoons julienne carrots
   1 1/2 cups heavy cream
   2 pounds Australian rock lobster tail meat,
      cut into 1" pieces
   3 tablespoons roughly chopped fresh mint leaves
   1 papaya, peeled, seeded and cut into slices lengthwise

Timbales:

Spinach Mousse:

   1 tablespoon butter, for greasing ramekins
   6 ounces fresh spinach leaves, washed and stems removed
   1/2 teaspoon chopped garlic
   1 egg
   1/2 cup heavy cream
   Salt and freshly ground pepper to taste

Carrot Mousse:

   6 ounces carrots, cut into chunks
   3 ounces butter
   2 cups chicken stock
   1 egg
   1/2 cup heavy cream
   Salt and freshly ground pepper to taste

1. Prepare spinach mousse: Purée spinach leaves and garlic in a food processor until quite smooth. Strain excess liquid from purée by squeezing it through cheesecloth. Return purée to food processor. With motor running, add egg and, when incorporated, add cream in a steady stream. Season with salt and pepper.

2. Prepare carrot mousse: In a saucepan, simmer carrots and butter in stock for about 25 minutes or until carrots are quite soft. Drain carrots, saving buttered stock for cooking other vegetables or for soup, and purée in a food processor until completely smooth. With motor running, add egg and, when incorporated, add cream in a steady stream. Season with salt and pepper.

(Continued on next page)

(Continued from previous page)

3. Prepare timbales: Butter 4 four-ounce ramekins. Fill half with spinach mousse and top with carrot mousse. Place in a water bath. Cover with foil and bake at 375 degrees until firmly set, about 15 minutes. Remove from oven and allow to sit for a few minutes. To unmold, run a knife around edges and invert.

4. Prepare lobster and sauce: In a large sauté pan, combine champagne, honey and carrots. Bring to a boil and reduce to 1/2 cup liquid. Add the cream and reduce to 1 1/2 cups liquid. Add the lobster and simmer until just cooked through. Add the mint at the very end.

5. Assembly: Unmold spinach and carrot mousse and center on 4 warm dinner plates. Surround with sauce and lobster meat, divided equally among the plates. Garnish each with 3 slices of papaya.

Charles Wiley

began cooking in 1973 in Lake Tahoe, California. His career has taken him to Alaska, San Francisco and Utah's Deer Valley Ski Resort and Stein Erikson Lodge at Park City. In 1989, he took over the kitchens of The Boulders Resort, broadening his innovative cooking style of intensely flavored dishes. As Carefree Resorts' executive chef, Charles is responsible for The Boulders' five dining choices and oversees the kitchens of The Peaks, Telluride, Colorado and Carmel Valley Resort, Carmel Valley, California. He was a scholarship recipient from Madeleine Kamman's School for American Chefs, selected as one of "America's Best Hotel Chefs" by the James Beard Foundation and chosen one of "America's Ten Best New Chefs" by "Food & Wine" in 1994.

When not in the resort's kitchens, Charles enjoys working out, riding his motorcycle, working on cars and cooking for his family. He is a sushi fan and loves chocolate. Says Charles about his food, "Never expect the expected. My food changes constantly."

Vegetarian Cabbage Rolls with Jicama Slaw, Spicy Pecans and Golden Tomato Corn Sauce

Makes 10 Servings

Spicy Pecans:
1/4 teaspoon cayenne pepper
1/4 teaspoon kosher salt
2 1/2 teaspoons chile powder
1/4 cup water
1 tablespoon honey
1/4 cup + 2 tablespoons sugar
1 cup whole pecans
2 cups peanut oil

Jicama Slaw:
1 jicama (approximately 16-ounces), peeled
2 red apples
1 small carrot
2 tablespoons fresh lime juice
2 tablespoons chopped chives
Kosher salt and freshly ground black pepper to taste

Golden Tomato Corn Sauce: (2 cups)
1 teaspoon olive oil
1/4 small onion, diced
1 large clove garlic, minced
1/3 cup white wine
1 tablespoon white wine vinegar
1/4 green bell pepper, seeded and diced
1 ear sweet corn, kernels shaved off the cob
2 medium yellow tomatoes, seeded and diced
1 bay leaf
1 cup vegetable stock
Kosher salt and freshly ground black pepper, to taste

Vegetarian Cabbage Rolls:
3 ears fresh sweet corn
1/4 cup cooked black beans
1 tablespoon olive oil
1/2 cup sun-dried tomatoes, sliced
1 poblano chile, roasted, seeded, peeled and diced
1 tablespoon minced cilantro
1 teaspoon minced fresh marjoram

(Continued on next page)

(Continued from previous page)

> 2 cloves garlic, roasted, peeled and chopped
> 1/2 teaspoon sherry vinegar
> 1 teaspoon fresh lemon juice
> 1 teaspoon fresh lime juice
> Kosher salt to taste
> 3/4 cup millet, cooked
> 1 1/2 cups water
> 5 carrots
> 10 cabbage leaves
> 3 tablespoons goat cheese

1. Prepare the spicy pecans: In a small bowl, combine cayenne pepper, salt and chile powder; mix well to incorporate. In a small skillet, combine the water, honey and sugar; boil until slightly thickened. Add pecans and cook 2 minutes; drain. Heat peanut oil until it registers 350 degrees on a deep fry thermometer. Add nuts and cook a minute or two, stirring occasionally. Remove with a wire skimmer and place in a stainless bowl. Quickly add chile seasoning and stir to coat. Pour out onto a baking sheet; separate the nuts. Allow to cool.

2. Prepare the jicama slaw: Julienne the jicama, apples and carrots. Combine all ingredients and mix well.

3. Prepare the golden tomato corn sauce: Heat oil in a saucepan over low heat and cook onion and garlic until translucent. Add wine; turn heat to high and reduce by half. Add vinegar, bell pepper, corn, tomatoes, bay leaf and vegetable stock; simmer approximately 20 minutes. Remove bay leaf, discard, and purée sauce in a blender; strain through a large-hole strainer into the pot. Bring back up to temperature, season with salt and pepper.

4. Prepare the cabbage rolls: Grill the corn-on-the-cob until slightly blackened; cut the kernels from the cob. Do not to cut too deeply. Combine the corn with the olive oil, sun-dried tomatoes, black beans, chiles, cilantro, marjoram, garlic, vinegar, lemon and lime juices and salt. Mix well and set aside. In a dry saucepan over medium-high heat, toast the millet until it pops and turns golden. Add water, cover and reduce heat to low. Cook until light and fluffy. Steam carrots for 35 minutes. Cool carrots for 5 minutes, allowing moisture to evaporate. Mash carrots, add millet, and fold into corn and black bean mixture. Adjust seasoning. Steam 10 nice cabbage leaves for 2 to 3 minutes and shock in ice water to halt cooking. Spoon 4 ounces of the vegetable mixture in each leaf and roll up. Steam 10 minutes just before serving.

6. Assembly: Slice warm cabbage rolls diagonally in half and arrange on plates. Spoon 1 1/2 ounces golden tomato corn sauce in front of roll. Sprinkle with 1 teaspoon of the goat cheese and arrange 3 pecan halves around the dish. Place 2 tablespoons of jicama slaw in the center of the cabbage roll halves.

Douglas Kent Hall ✦ *"Jim Morrison — The Doors"*
Black and White Photography

Kevin Sloan ✦ *"The Garden Memorial"*

Acrylic on Canvas   24" x 20"

Marc Jasper D'Ambrosi ✦ *"Love Anchor"*
Bronze   36" x 10" x 10"

John Dawson ✦ *"Savanna Time"*

Oil on Canvas   60" x 72"

David Bradley ✦ *"Indian Country Today"*

Acrylic on Canvas   72" x 60"

Bob "Daddy-O" Wade ✦ *"Cowgirl and the Paint"*
Acrylic on Photo Linen   36" x 60"

Mario Romero Mauricio ✦ *"Niño Caballero"*
Acrylic on Paper   21 1/2" x 30"

Anne Coe ✦ *"Monkey Business"*

Acrylic on Canvas   50" x 70"

Thomas Coffin ✦ *"Idol Series"*

Aluminum and Limestone   47" x 11" x 7"

Rudy Fernandez ✦ *"Unveiling"*

Mixed Media   16" x 12"

Howard Post ♦ *"Roundup Crew"*

Oil on Canvas   56" x 44"

James Holmes ✦ *"Border Radio"*
Mixed Media   18" x 24" x 12"

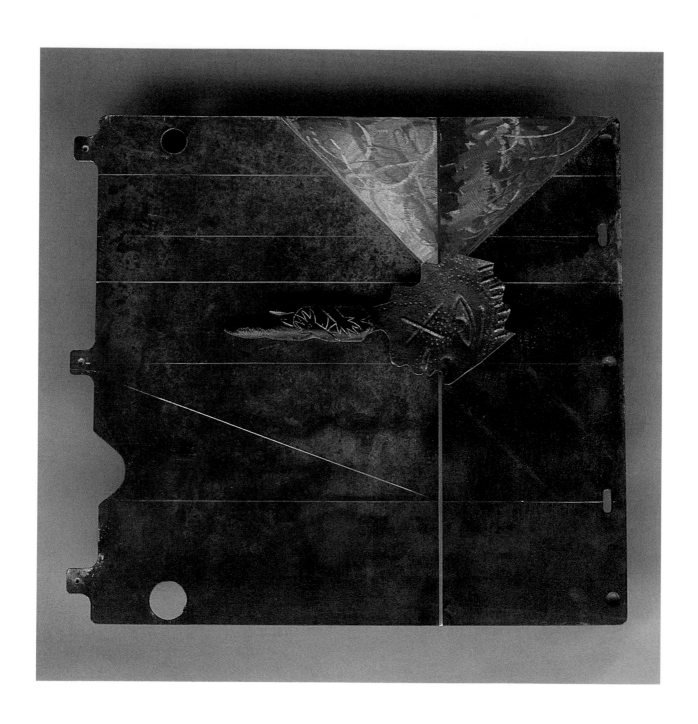

Joe Willie Smith ✦ *"Coming to America"*
Metal and Bakelite   16 3/4" x 15" x 2"

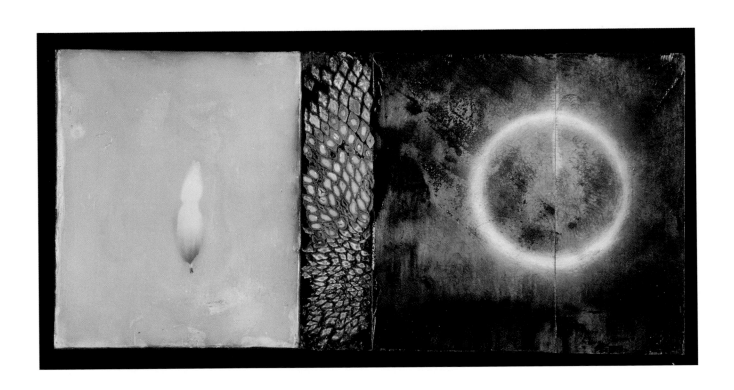

Mayme Kratz ✦ *"Cleave"*

Oil, Wax, Sunflower 5" x 10"

Earl Linderman ♦ *"Last Plane from Casablanca"*
Oil on Canvas   84" x 72"

Thomas A. Philabaum ✦ *"Drinking with the Devil"*

Glass   8" x 8" x 22"

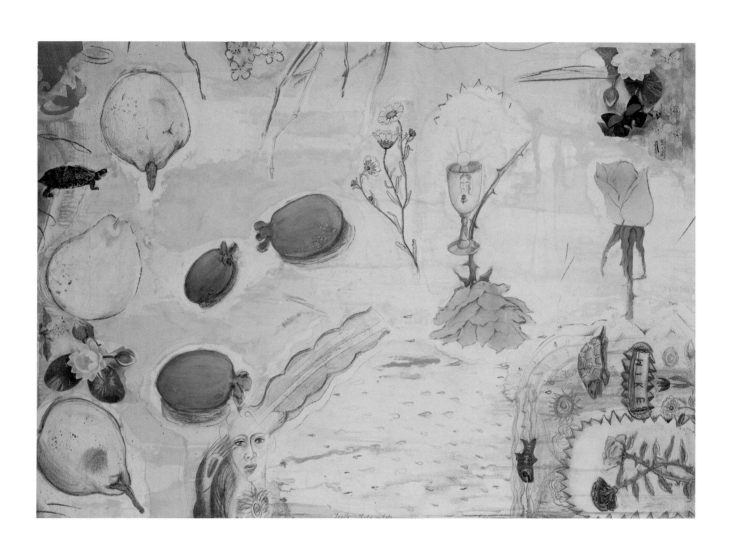

Kathryn Kain ✦ *"Turtle tête à tête"*

Monotype Collage   19" x 26"

DESSERTS

Food styling -- Bobbi Jo & Razz Kamnitzer   *Photography -- Bob Carey*

Jean-Michel Boulot

says he might have become an artist — sculpting or drawing — had he not become a chef. I used to draw a lot before I started in this business. But now I compensate my lack of time for drawing into my work. It's part of my signature. Everything I do has to be very artistic or it doesn't have any appeal to me."

Jean-Michel started working in kitchens at the age of fifteen, so he "could travel all over the world." And travel, he did. His culinary addresses include the Restaurant Le Jules Vernes and Hotel Hilton International in Paris; Restaurant Le Beaujolais in Vancouver, Canada; Hotel Sofitel in San Francisco, Hilton International at Lert Park in Bangkok, Thailand; and Hilton Hawaiian Village in Honolulu, Hawaii. He joined the Ritz-Carlton in Palm Beach as sous chef and became executive chef of the Ritz-Carlton in Phoenix in 1994. Presently, Jean-Michel and his staff are in the process of revamping the fine dining and grill menus at Desert Highlands.

Sinful Fingers

Makes approximately sixteen 1x4-inch fingers

- 3 ounces water
- 7 ounces unsalted butter
- 2 1/2 tablespoons granulated sugar
- 1 pound semisweet chocolate, chopped
- 3 whole large eggs
- 1 large egg yolk
- 3/4 cup semisweet chocolate chips
- 1/4 cup whipping cream
- 1/4 cup lightly toasted hazelnuts, crushed

1. Preheat oven to 350 degrees. Combine water, butter and sugar; bring to a boil. Pour boiling liquid mixture over chopped chocolate in a mixing bowl. Whisk until chocolate is thoroughly melted. Add whole eggs and yolk and whisk until blended.

2. Prepare an 8x8-inch baking pan by spraying with nonstick cooking spray. Line bottom with parchment paper. Pour mixture into pan and spread evenly. Bake for 20 to 25 minutes until mixture sets. Chill torte, remove from pan, invert and remove paper.

3. Gently boil the cream and pour it over the chocolate chips. Whisk until smooth. Spread chocolate mixture on top of torte and chill torte.

4. Remove torte from refrigerator. Cut torte in half. Cut each half into slices 1-inch wide. Dip ends of the fingers into the crushed hazelnuts.

Mango Crème Brûlée

Makes 8 Servings

    5 1/2 ounces granulated sugar
    3 cups heavy cream
    8 egg yolks
    1 cup mango purée

1. Preheat oven to 275 degrees. Lightly butter 8 ramekins and set aside.
2. Bring sugar and cream to a boil. Meanwhile, whisk egg yolks and mango purée in a large bowl.
2. Slowly pour hot cream into egg yolk mixture, whisking constantly.
3. Place ramekins in a shallow baking dish; pour cream/egg yolk mixture into the ramekins. Pour enough hot water into the baking dish to come halfway up the ramekins.
4. Bake in the water bath for approximately 45 minutes or until set.
5. To serve: Sprinkle the top of each brûlée with granulated sugar. Place under a broiler until sugar caramelizes.

Judy Capertina *says, "I was actually a bio-chem major in college. I was going for (a degree in) medical technology." But, after visiting a friend who lived in Hyde Park, New York — the site of the Culinary Institute of America — she says she became very interested in the school and "ended up going."*

Graduating from the CIA in 1978, Judy's recent culinary addresses prior to arriving at The Phoenician have included the Grand Hyatt Wailea Hotel and Resort, Maui, Hawaii; The Inn and Links at Spanish Bay, Pebble Beach, California; and the Princeville Hotel and Resort, Kauai, Hawaii. She has been featured in "Bon Appetit" (June 1994) and received numerous awards for her pastry work, including First Place for sugar and chocolate work in a competition at the Chicago Ritz-Carlton in 1994.

Judy likes Thai and Oriental foods, especially Vietnamese dishes. Away from creating pastry delights, she says, "I'm very much into dance and martial arts, tae kwon do." When asked what people should know about her, she says, "I feel it's my responsibility to teach my art to those who work for me."

Dino
DeBell *has a diverse background in restaurant management and distribution. His experiences have taken him from his home in Denver, Colorado, to Hawaii and California before arriving at The Lodge at Vail.*

While at The Lodge, Dino worked with former Lodge chef, James Cohen, now executive chef of The Phoenician Resort in Scottsdale, Arizona. Dino has been chef de cuisine at the Lodge's Cucina Rustica restaurant and sous chef of The Wildflower, also at The Lodge. He recently spent some time refining his Italian cuisine background at Tra Vigne, in Napa Valley, with its nationally known chef, Michael Chiarello. Dino was promoted to executive chef in June of 1996.

Dino comes from a food-oriented family: His father had a small Italian restaurant in Denver and his uncle is an importer of specialty foods. When not in the resort's kitchen — which is a rarity — he likes to fly fish and travel. Dino says he favors southern Italian dishes, for their "bigger, bolder flavors," and had he not become a chef, civil engineering would have been his career path.

Sabiossa (Pound Cake) with Strawberry Compote

Makes 6 to 8 Servings

Sabiossa:
  1 1/4 pounds unsalted butter
  2 1/2 cups granulated sugar
  6 whole eggs
  1 1/2 tablespoons vanilla
  1/2 cup dark rum
  3 1/4 teaspoons baking powder
  1 1/4 pounds potato starch (potato flour; available at specialty grocers)

Creme Paticcera (pastry cream):
  2 cups milk
  1 cup sugar
  7 egg yolks
  1 whole egg
  4 tablespoons all-purpose flour
  1 tablespoon vanilla
  4 ounces unsalted butter
  2 cups heavy cream, whipped (optional)

Strawberry Compote:
  2 pints fresh strawberries, quartered
  1 tablespoon sugar
  1 teaspoon aged balsamic vinegar

1. Prepare the sabiossa: Preheat the oven to 350 degrees. Butter and flour an 8-inch tube pan. Cream together the butter and sugar until smooth. Add eggs, a few at a time. Dissolve baking powder in rum and add to creamed mixture. Add potato starch and mix only until smooth — **do not overmix.** Pour batter into pan and bake for 30 minutes, or until firm and tests dry on a toothpick.

2. Prepare the creme paticcera: In a saucepan heat the milk and half of the sugar. In a bowl, mix the eggs with the remaining sugar, add the flour and mix until smooth. Add hot milk to egg mixture and return to heat until mixture thickens, stirring constantly. Remove from heat and stir in vanilla and butter until melted. Cool. When cooled a bit, add the whipped heavy cream, if desired, for a lighter pastry cream.

3. Prepare the compote: Mix all the ingredients together and set aside.

4. Assembly: Slice the sabiossa into approximately 1 inch slices; three slices per serving. Spoon creme paticcera onto slices and top with strawberry compote.

Bread Pudding with Amaretto Sauce

Makes 6 Servings
   4 cups milk
   1/4 cup semolina flour
   2 eggs
   4 cups condensed milk
   1 tablespoon vanilla extract
   9 cups cubed white bread
   3 cups peeled and cubed mangoes

Amaretto Sauce:
   3/4 cup milk
   3/4 cup heavy cream
   4 eggs
   1/2 cup sugar
   1 1/2 teaspoons vanilla extract
   2 tablespoons amaretto
   Mango slices for garnish (optional)

1. Prepare the bread pudding: Preheat the oven to 250 degrees. In a saucepan, bring milk to a boil. Add semolina and whisk constantly until the mixture thickens to a cream consistency. Remove from heat and whip milk mixture with an electric mixer on low speed for 1 minute. Add eggs, condensed milk and vanilla extract. Reserve mixture.

2. Put 1 1/2 cups of bread cubes and 1/2 cup of mangoes into each of 6 individual (16-ounce) soufflé dishes. Cover with 1/2 cup of the milk mixture. Set dishes in a deep baking pan filled with hot water to within 3/4-inch of the top of the soufflé dishes. Bake for 45 minutes or until bread pudding is slightly firm to the touch. Cool for 30 minutes before serving.

3. Prepare the sauce: In a saucepan, heat milk and cream to a boil. Remove from heat and reserve. In a mixing bowl, stir together eggs and sugar. Pour egg mixture into a separate saucepan. Gradually pour hot milk mixture into egg mixture over low heat; bring to a simmer. Pour into a clean bowl; chill over ice. Stir in vanilla and amaretto. Pass amaretto sauce separately to spoon over bread pudding.

Michael DeMaria *loves desserts and says, "My favorite dessert is on the menu at T. Cooks, Bread Pudding with Amaretto Sauce. I like more cakey, ice creamy style things. I love different shortcakes, breads and fruit sauces. I believe that desserts should have different components: something soft, something creamy, something fruity and something crispy."*

Read more about Michael on page 52.

Vincent Guerithault's *cookbook, titled "Vincent's Cookbook," (Ten Speed Press) features recipes for many of his popular dishes at the restaurant which bears his name.*

About desserts, he writes, "A lot of people say that they swear off desserts at the end of a meal, but we certainly haven't found that to be true at Vincent's. I like to think it's because we serve desserts that they won't find anywhere else and that ours are irresistible."

Read more about Vincent on page 55.

Chocolate Macadamia Tart with Warm Chocolate Grand Marnier Sauce

Makes 4 Servings

>   4 ounces semisweet chocolate
>   4 ounces butter
>   3 eggs
>   2 ounces all-purpose flour
>   6 ounces sugar
>   1 cup macadamia nuts, whole

Chocolate Grand Marnier Sauce:

>   4 ounces semisweeet chocolate
>   2 ounces whole milk
>   2 ounces Grand Marnier

1. Cut chocolate into small pieces and melt with butter over low heat.
2. Separate eggs. Whisk egg yolks and add to chocolate mixture, blending well.
3. In a separate bowl, whip egg whites with sugar; add flour and whole macadamia nuts. Pour into individual, buttered tart shells (approximately 3-inches in diameter).
4. Bake at 350 degrees for about 15 minutes.
5. Make sauce: Break chocolate into small pieces and melt over low heat with milk. When melted, slowly add Grand Marnier.
6. Spoon sauce over tarts.

Lemon Curd Cake
with Fresh Berries

Makes 10 Servings

Génoise:
  1/3 cup sugar
  2 large eggs
  1/2 cup all-purpose flour

Lemon Curd:
  3/4 cup fresh lemon juice
  1 1/3 cups sugar
  4 eggs
  2 gelatin leaves, soaked in cold water (available at gourmet
    or bakery supply shops; or substitute 1 1/4 teaspoons
    powdered gelatin, dissolved in 1/4 cup cold water)
  10 ounces unsalted butter, softened and cut in small pieces

Garnish:
  1 cup crème fraîche
  Fresh seasonal berries

Gerald Hirigoyen *began his culinary career at the age of 13 in a bake shop. He says he began with pastry making because he did not find a suitable opening at a restaurant. Gerald believes by beginning with pastry, which he feels is good for mastering techniques, a move to cooking can be made later. "It's harder to go the other way," he says.*

Read more about Gerald on page 56.

1. Prepare génoise: Preheat oven to 400 degrees. Butter and flour a 9-inch springform pan and set aside. In a large heatproof bowl, combine sugar and eggs. Place over simmering water and whisk until just lukewarm. Remove from the heat and, using a mixer on high speed, beat until cool, about 12 minutes. Sift flour over the batter and fold in. Pour into the prepared pan; smooth the top. Bake about 15 to 18 minutes. Invert on rack, remove pan and let cool completely.

2. Prepare lemon curd: In a stainless steel mixing bowl, combine lemon juice, sugar and eggs. Place bowl directly over medium heat; whisk until mixture just begins to boil. Reduce heat to low; continue whisking briskly for two more minutes. Remove bowl from heat and immediately add gelatin leaves; combine well. With a mixer on high speed, whip until mixture cools slightly, about 2 minutes. Reduce speed to medium, add butter and continue mixing until smooth, about 2 to 3 minutes.

3. Assembly: Carefully slice génoise into 2 layers. Pour 1/3 of the lemon mixture evenly over the bottom of a 9 x 1 1/2-inch springform pan. Top with a génoise layer. Repeat lemon curd and génoise layers, ending with a lemon curd. Cover and refrigerate until set, about 2 to 3 hours. Serve with fresh berries and a dollop of crème fraîche.

Chrysa

Kaufman *studied art and art history in college "just because everyone thought I was talented." After discovering cooking, though, she was hooked and spent eight years with C. Steele & Company Marketplace. Chrysa fine-tuned her culinary skills in California with Nancy Silverton and Mark Peel at their restaurant, Campanile, and as a cook at Terra in Napa California.*

In 1993, Chrysa and her husband, Tom, fulfilled a dream by opening their own restaurant, Rancho Pinot Grill. Its changing menu features dishes prepared with the freshest, organic ingredients available, utilizing local growers as much as possible. "I need the very freshest ingredients to produce the simple, straightforward, flavorful results I strive for in my cooking. And, I want to encourage sustainable local agriculture. My cooking by nature is very seasonal. You get the best products, the freshest products during their own natural seasons."

Chrysa really goes for Vietnamese and Thai food. "I love the clean but intense flavors." And when it comes to dessert, it's ice cream, "really good coffee or espresso ice cream." She spends her time out of the kitchen gardening and fly fishing. "I just worship fly fishing."

Orange Yogurt Cake with Fresh Berries

Makes 6 to 8 Servings

Syrup:
Juice of 2 medium oranges
2 tablespoons fresh lemon juice
2 tablespoons sugar

Cake:
Zest of 2 medium oranges
2 ounces unsalted butter
2/3 cup sugar
1 egg
1/2 cup yogurt, do not use nonfat or low-fat
1 1/4 cups all-purpose flour
3/4 teaspoon baking powder
1/4 teaspoon baking soda
Pinch of salt

Garnish:
Fresh blueberries
1/2 cup crème fraîche (sour cream can be substituted)

1. Prepare the syrup: Combine the orange and lemon juices and the sugar in a small saucepan. Simmer over low heat for about 2 minutes. Set aside.

2. Prepare the cake: Preheat the oven to 350 degrees. Finely mince the orange zest. Using a mixer, cream together the butter, sugar and zest until light. Add the egg and beat until incorporated. In a separate bowl, combine the flour, baking powder, baking soda and salt. Using the mixer at low speed, add the flour mixture alternately with the yogurt to the creamed mixture. Butter and flour an 8-inch springform pan and pour the batter into the prepared pan. Bake for 35 to 45 minutes until golden. Remove from oven and, while the cake is still hot, pierce the entire top of the cake with a skewer and spoon the orange syrup evenly over the top. Cool the cake in the pan.

4. Serve individual slices with fresh blueberries and a dollop of crème fraîche.

David Bierk ✦ *"Eulogy to Earth, Still Life, to Espinosa"*

Oil on Canvas   72" x 72"

Lyle London ✦ *"Oracle #2"*

Copper   8' x 4'6" x 2'6"

Kevin Irvin ✦ *"Eclipse"*

Mixed Media on Canvas   14" x 14"

John Armstrong ✦ *"Untitled"*

Welded Steel   50" x 52" x 6"

Kathryn Jacobi ✦ *"Diva in Extremis"*
Oil on Panel   16" x 12"

Bill Schenck ✦ *"Gone with the Gunsmoke"*
Oil on Canvas   50" x 40"

Mark McDowell ✦ *"St. Florian"*

Oil on Canvas   60" x 36"

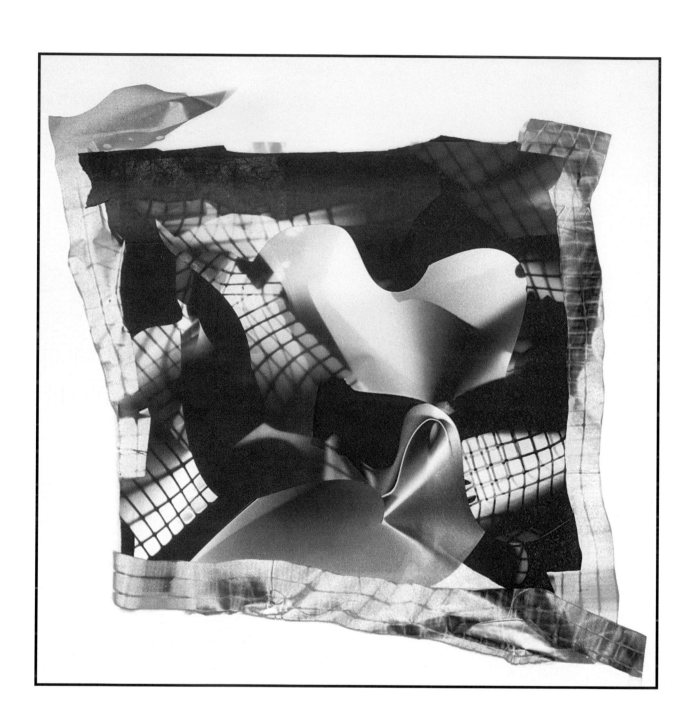

Larry Bell ✦ *"SMS #327"*
Mixed Media on Canvas   30" x 30"

Carlos Aguilar Linares ✦ *"El Mago - The Magician"*

Bronze   76 x 43 x 21 cm

Bill Barrett ✦ *"Guardia"*

Fabricated Bronze   102" H x 72" W x 72" D

Francisco Lopez (OCHOA) ✦ *"Vendedora de Flores"*

Monotype   30" x 22"

Karl Dowhie ✦ *"Triple Alcoves - Colorado River, Grand Canyon"*
Acrylic on Canvas   36" x 48"

Edward "Rusty" Walker ✦ *"Navajo Rugs"*

Oil on Canvas   50" x 66"

Tom Ortega ✦ *"Animal Crackers"*

Mixed Media on Wood   16" x 26"

Stephen Britko ✦ *"The Window Series"*

Mixed Media   24" x 30"

Mel Roman ✦ *"God Bless America"*

Duratran Print   72" x 48"

Cinnamon Apple & Raisin Crisp

Makes 6 Servings

   3 pounds Granny Smith or Golden Delicious apples
   2 tablespoons raisins
   1 tablespoon lemon juice
   6 tablespoons unsalted butter, divided use
   5 tablespoons plus 1/4 cup sugar, divided use
   1 tablespoon rum
   1/2 cup all-purpose flour
   1/2 teaspoon cinnamon
   8 sheets phyllo dough
   Melted butter for brushing on sheets

1. Peel, quarter and core apples; cut into 1/8-inch thick slices. Toss apples with raisins and lemon juice in a bowl. Heat 1 tablespoon butter over medium-high heat; add apple/raisin mixture and sauté for about 5 minutes. Add 5 tablespoons sugar and rum; sauté for another 5 minutes or until apple slices are tender. Transfer to a platter and let cool.

2. In the bowl of a food processor, place flour, cinnamon, remaining sugar and butter. Pulse-blend mixture to form coarse crumbs; remove to a parchment lined baking sheet. Refrigerate mixture for 15 minutes.

3. Preheat oven to 375 degrees.

4. Brush a phyllo sheet generously with melted butter and lay flat on a buttered 9-inch pie pan; edges should overhang pie pan. Repeat with remaining phyllo sheets and butter. Spoon apple/raisin mixture onto sheets on the pie pan. Fold edges of phyllo sheets over filling and cover with cinnamon mixture.

5. Bake in oven 20 to 25 minutes. The cinnamon crisp topping should be lightly browned, the phyllo golden in color.

Hubert Keller, *a French native, was trained by Paul Haeberlin, Paul Bocuse and Roger Verge before coming to the United States and San Francisco in 1982. He loves desserts and about this recipe he says, "I love this delicious apple and raisin crisp. Serve it warm or at room temperature, just as is or with a blond caramel sauce, vanilla ice cream, whipped cream or even apricot compote, and you are halfway to heaven."*

Read more about Hubert on page 59.

Don Pintabona *has been an integral part of the success of the acclaimed Tribeca Grill since the restaurant's beginning in 1990. His innovative American fare is the result of his international culinary travels. After graduating in 1982 from the Culinary Institute of America, Don took a five month tasting tour of Europe, where he honed his culinary skills as well. He began applying Asian techniques and spices to his cooking style after sojourns to Japan and the Far East.*

Returning to New York, Don trained with some of New York's notable chefs, including Charles Palmer, The River Cafe and Aureole; and Daniel Boulud of Le Regencé in the Plaza Athenée. He lectures on "Banquet Preparation and Execution" at Cornell's School of Hotel Management and instructs culinary courses at The New School in Manhattan. He has also hosted many elite New York dinners, including President Clinton's fund-raising dinner for the 1992 Democratic Convention.

Don has demonstrated his recipes and healthy cooking techniques on television, including the TV Food Network. His recipes and cooking tips have been featured in publications such as "Food & Wine," "Gourmet," "Bon Appetit," "New York Magazine" and "The New York Times."

Pear Fritters

Makes 4 Servings
   4 Bartlett pears, peeled
   1/2 vanilla bean
   2 quarts water
   2 cups sugar
   Oil for frying

Fritter Batter:
   7 ounces all-purpose flour
   1 cup white wine
   1 tablespoon vegetable oil
   3 eggs, separated
   Pinch of salt
   1 1/2 ounces sugar
   1/2 teaspoon baking powder

Garnish:
   Powdered sugar
   Vanilla ice cream

1. Prepare the pears: Combine the water, sugar and vanilla bean in a saucepan. Add pears and bring to a boil. Remove from heat and cover pears and let sit until cool.

2. Prepare the batter: Combine the flour, white wine, oil, egg yolks, salt and baking powder; mix thoroughly. Beat egg whites until frothy, add the sugar and continue beating until the whites hold stiff peaks. Fold egg whites into batter until smooth.

3. Prepare the fritters: Slice pears in half and core. Section each half into 4 or 5 wedges. Dip pears into the batter and fry in 350-degree oil until golden brown. Sprinkle with powdered sugar and serve with vanilla ice cream.

Chocolate Almond Madeleines

Makes 2 dozen

    1 8-ounce can almond paste
    3 eggs
    4 tablespoons butter, melted
    1/4 cup sweetened cocoa

1. Preheat oven to 350 degrees. Spray madeleine molds with nonstick vegetable spray.

2. Using an electric mixer, work the almond paste and eggs until very smooth and light. Add cocoa and mix to combine well, scraping down the sides of the bowl. Slowly mix in the melted butter.

3. Scrape the mixture into a pastry bag fitted with a plain tip and pipe the dough into the madeleine molds (alternatively, spoon the dough into the molds), filling each mold 3/4 full.

4. Bake for 10 minutes or until cakes are springy to the touch. Remove from the oven and turn the madeleines out onto a cake rack. Cool completely. Store madeleines in an airtight container.

Richard Ruskell *has a master's degree in fine arts from Western Illinois University, Macomb, Illinois, and is a graduate of the French Culinary Institute in New York City. He began his professional pastry journey in Cannes, France, at the Hotel Gray d'Albion, where he worked with executive chef Jacques Chibois in the kitchens of Le Royal Gray Restaurant.*

Richard has received many awards for his pastry creations, including 1996 top honors at the Domaine Carneros Wedding Cake Competition in the "celebrity cakes" category with his "Dr. Jekyll and Mrs. Hyde" entry. He has also received laudatory ink in "Pastry Art & Design" magazine (Autumn, 1995). His Phoenician Crunch Cake is featured in "Grand Finales: The Art of The Plated Dessert," a book published by the editors of "Chocolatier" and "Pastry Art & Design."

Certainly a pastry chef extraordinaire, Richard has a preference for "Minnesota comfort food." When not creating intricate delicacies, he likes to build model ships. Had he not become a pastry chef, Richard says he would be more involved with acting. During the time he lived in New York City, Richard appeared on a few "soaps."

Richard Ruskell — **The Phoenician** *— Scottsdale, Arizona*

Carlos Aguilar Linares has always known he was going to be an artist, in some manner. "I am certain I should be an artist," he says. "I played the piano, it was my job, and my hobby was to make sculptures. One day I realized that everything had changed. My job or my work was to make sculptures and my hobby was to play the piano."

Carlos says he believes the change came about as his son began to grow. He realized he did not want to continue traveling, playing piano with a band.

Carlos' sculptures have appeared in many exhibitions, including Three Key Awards, International Festival of Jazz, Bern, Switzerland; Otro Lugar de La Mancha, Polanco, Mexico; Tavern on the Green, New York, New York; Museum of National History, Mexico City, Mexico; and Centro Cultural Teresa Carreno, Caracas, Venezuela.

Carlos says his sculptures "create thought." As an example, he says his sculpture of a magician shows cascading playing cards, the magician's hat and the magician's hands, but no magician. Another sculpture features the illusion of a man playing chess. Carlos, however, shows only the man's hands.

About his work, Carlos says, "People can make up stories about my work; it's not just pretty like a decoration."

John Armstrong knew from an early age he would be involved with art. "I thought when I was in the sixth grade I was going to teach art (he later did teach for awhile). I guess it's always been art," he says. "I would liked to have played Major League Baseball, but I didn't have the skill for that. Or maybe I'd have been a house builder."

John's education includes Eastern Montana College, Billings, Montana and the University of Montana, Missoula, Montana. His career has taken him from teaching high school art classes in Montana to the Visual Arts Manager of the Scottsdale Center for the Arts (1975-1980), Scottsdale, Arizona. Since 1980, he can be found at Armstrong-Prior, Inc., printers, publishers, consultants. His work has been exhibited in various public collections including the University of Montana, Billings and Missoula; C.M. Russell Art Museum, Great Falls, Montana; and Del Webb Corporation — Terravita, Scottsdale. Says John about his work, "It comes from the influence of my environment."

John is an avid Phoenix Suns' fan and likes to read and hike. He refers to his palate as cosmopolitan and professes a strong liking of spicy foods — Cajun and Thai. He describes himself as a "creative problem solver."

Carlos Aguilar Linares

John Armstrong

Bill Barrett's days are pretty well filled with painting, printing, sculpting and making jewelry. It's a life with which he's familiar. "My father was an artist," he says. "I'm an artist. I have two sons who are artists and a daughter that's a film maker. So, it's in the family. We've always been involved in the arts."

Bill's education includes a bachelor's and master's degree in science and a master's degree in fine arts from the University of Michigan. His work has appeared in many exhibitions, including Cline Fine Art Gallery, Santa Fe, New Mexico; Kouros Gallery and Flat Iron Gallery, both in New York, New York; DeGraaf Fine Art, Chicago, Illinois; and Kyoto Gallery, Kyoto, Japan. Bill's work is also among many collections, such as those at the Scottsdale Center for the Arts, Scottsdale, Arizona; Virginia Museum of Fine Arts, Richmond, Virginia; University of Hartford, Hartford, Connecticut; and the International Foundation Art Gallery, Sofia, Bulgaria.

"I do mainly welded, cast bronze sculptures," he says. "They're of an abstract nature." Bill professes to rarely cook, but can whip up his favorite, "Welsh rarebit with shrimp and pasta over rice." About himself he says, "I'm pretty easygoing. I like to play golf and I like working, keeping myself busy."

John Battenberg says he has absolutely no idea what he'd do had he not become an artist. "I started as a little kid and never varied." He did, though, mention being a handyman, because he has "Yankee cleverness."

John is "very concerned with the environment, the earth and the nature of things." His concern, he says, is reflected in his work. He describes himself as "a contemporary shaman mystic. I think artists are shamans and I think they're the last of the connection with our ancient ancestors."

John's education includes the Ruskin School, Oxford University, England; a master's in fine arts from Michigan State University, East Lansing, Michigan; and graduate work at California College of Arts and Crafts, Oakland, California. His work has appeared in solo exhibitions including the Fresno Art Museum, Fresno, California; Harcourts Modern and Contemporary Art and Academy of Art, both in San Francisco, California. Among his group exhibitions is "Fifty Years: A Syntex Retrospective," Syntex Corporation, Palo Alto, California (1995). John's work also appears in collections at Commune de Pietrasanta, Lucca, Italy; the Royal British War Museum, London, England; and the Smithsonian in Washington, D.C.

Bill Barrett

John Battenberg

Larry Bell says if he had to get a "real" job, he doesn't know what he'd do. He had set out to be a cartoonist. However, after taking a batch of "strange and bizarre" courses involving a great deal of theory, he realized he wasn't going to be a cartoonist.

Larry's work has appeared in many solo exhibitions, including Tampa Museum of Art, Tampa, Florida; Tucson Museum of Art, Tucson, Arizona; Tony Shafrazi Gallery, New York, New York; and Musee d'Art Contemporain, Lyon, France. Group exhibitions include High Museum of Art, Atlanta, Georgia; Solomon R. Guggenheim Museum, New York; and Rufino Tamayo Museum, Mexico City, Mexico.

About his work, Larry provided the following statement: "Each studio investigation is arrived at by the previous one. Spontaneity, intuition and improvisation are the three key elements my work thrives on. It's kept open all the time. I work quickly, without a lot of contemplation of what goes where."

Among his awards and recognitions, Larry is the recipient of the Governors Award for Excellence and Achievement in the Arts (Visual Arts), State of New Mexico, 1990.

David Bierk has always been interested in art. However, until he was nineteen years old, his career goal was to be a second baseman in the major leagues. Then a major league scout clued him about his shortcomings and he traded in the baseball bat for a paintbrush.

David's studies include Humboldt State University, Arcata, California, BA and MFA; and California College of Arts and Crafts, Oakland, California.

His work has appeared in many exhibitions, including recent solo showings at Leedy-Voulkos Galleries, Kansas City, Missouri; Lisa Kurts Gallery, Memphis, Tennessee; and Diane Farris Gallery, Vancouver, British Columbia. David's work is also among several public collections, including the National Gallery of Canada, Ottawa, Ontario; Grand Hyatt Hotel, Hong Kong; and Harvard Law School, Harvard University, Cambridge, Massachusetts.

About his work, David says, "I pay homage to, and have really a love for, art of the past that communicated the kind of virtues art always stood for, like beauty, humanism, heroism. My work is really a critique on modernism and I find a lot of those things lacking in contemporary art and life."

About himself, he says, "I remain an explorer. I still have a tremendous passion and energy for painting. But I'm also embracing and celebrating life through my art and through my

Larry Bell

David Bierk

David Bradley is also a writer. "I've done a couple of children's books, illustrations and all." He also has an interest in becoming a private investigator. "I'm trying to get my license," he says. "It's part of my novel. I want to be able to say I was one so I know what I'm talking about." The novel, he says, should be finished the fall of 1998.

David's education includes the Institute of American Indian Arts, Santa Fe, New Mexico; and a bachelor's degree in fine arts from the College of Santa Fe, Santa Fe. His work has appeared at such exhibitions as "Art and the Law," West Publishing, St. Paul, Minnesota (1994); and "Contemporary Artists of New Mexico," City Hall Gallery, Guadalajara, Mexico (1994). Additionally, David's work can be viewed in collections at The Museum of Fine Arts, Santa Fe; The Heard Museum, Phoenix, Arizona; and the Plains Art Museum, Fargo, North Dakota.

About his work, David says, "It sometimes deals with political issues. The majority of the work I'm known for does have political commentary. It's allegorical, narrative."

Stephen Britko will most likely be with his horses when not in his studio creating — "raising and riding and doing some training." He enjoys the outdoors tremendously and says, "That's why I enjoy horses so much, being able to ride in the mountains. I like my solitude."

He goes for any kind of Italian food, and when asked what he'd be doing had he not become an artist, he says, "I've never thought about it because this is all I've ever wanted to do."

Stephen's education includes the Tamarind Institute, University of New Mexico, Albuquerque, New Mexico; Southern Illinois University, Carbondale, Illinois, and McKendree College, in Lebanon, Illinois. His work has been exhibited at Fort Lewis College, Durango, Colorado; the Linda Durham Gallery in Santa Fe, New Mexico and a solo exhibition at the Munson Gallery, also in Santa Fe. Other work appears in the public collections of the Evansville Museum of Art, Evansville, Indiana and the Standard Oil Corporate Collections in Chicago, Illinois.

Also a printer, he put his artwork on hold for a few years. Today, he says. "I'm back doing my own work. I've many, many ideas built up over the years. So, it's constantly exploring and changing."

David Bradley

Stephen Britko

Anne Coe says she would have been involved in genetics and science had she not become an artist. "You know, [artists and scientists] are not really that far apart. We're both trying to explain things, we just use a different language to do it." Opting for art, her education includes Arizona State University, Tempe, Arizona and Universidad de Puerto Rico, San Juan, Puerto Rico.

When not creating, Anne gives her attention to her "serious avocations." She runs a non-profit land trust in the Superstition Springs area where she is working to preserve the Sonoran desert wilderness.

Her art has appeared in solo exhibitions such as "Seven Deadly Sins and Other Transgressions" at the Scottsdale Center for the Arts, Scottsdale, Arizona (1992) and in group exhibitions, including "Art and the Law," a traveling exhibit (1994).

"My work comes from my heart. It's about things that I care deeply and passionately about. It's serious work but not necessarily solemn. It has a joy of life in it, though I don't steer away from the harder issues. It is about life and living things and life on earth and all the things I love."

Anne says of herself, "I think of myself as a self-actualizing individual. Someone that sees a problem, whether in my work or my personal life, and I act upon that. I find solutions. That's the ultimate creative personality. I'm creative in every aspect of my life."

Thomas Coffin says he would probably have gone into archaeology had he not become an artist. "I like ancient stuff," he says. "But I started drawing when I was three, so it never entered into my mind to do anything else."

His education includes the Institute of American Indian Arts, Santa Fe, New Mexico; and a bachelor's in fine arts from the Kansas City Art Institute, Kansas City, Misourri. He worked at the Shidoni Fine Art Foundry in Santa Fe, before pursuing his present career as a sculptor, painter and architectural restorer. Tom was commissioned in 1988 to sculpt four life-size bronzes for McDonald's corporate headquarters in Chicago and has worked on various restoration projects in New York City, including Carnegie Hall.

Tom recently returned to the Southwest, making Phoenix his home. He has a 1967 Plymouth Sport convertible and likes to travel. He has been commissioned to build a Route 66 monument for the State of New Mexico Highway Commission and New Mexico Arts Division. It will be erected in Tucumcari, New Mexico, in the spring of 1997.

Anne Coe

Thomas Coffin

Joel Coplin says he knew he was going to become an artist when he met his teacher. "I met Frank Mason in New York. He's a classical artist, world renowned and a big, booming, inspiring guy. When I met him, I said that's what I want to do. That was in 1977." Joel was in New York at that time to learn about furniture design and how to work with wood. After meeting Mason, he says, "I threw it all down the drain and started studying painting."

Joel studied at The Art Student's League of New York, New York. His work has appeared in many exhibitions including "Truth & Fantasy," Lisa Sette Gallery, Scottsdale, Arizona (1995); "Southwest 96," Museum of Fine Arts, Santa Fe, New Mexico (1996); "Directors Choice," Scottsdale Center for the Arts, Scottsdale, Arizona (1995); and the Butler Institute of American Art, Youngstown, Ohio.

When asked what people should know about his work, Joel says, "It belongs on their walls. I'm a figurative painter and I've got a bunch of figures that need homes."

Incidentally, Joel did learn woodworking and cabinet making. Not only does he frame all his own work, but he recently completed building a kitchen for his wife.

Philip C. Curtis originally planned to be a lawyer. "I went to law school; I had one year at the University of Michigan. My father was a lawyer," says Philip. "I thought I could probably make a living if I became a lawyer."

Then, he found out about the art world. He says, "I grew up in a town that didn't have a breath of art. I only saw a couple of paintings in my life until I got to college."

Philip's education includes Albion College, Albion, Michigan, and the University of Michigan, Ann Arbor, Michigan, where he achieved a Bachelor of Arts degree, and Yale School of Fine Arts, New Haven, Connecticut. His work has appeared in such solo exhibitions as "And Time Stood Still," Riva Yares Gallery, Scottsdale, Arizona (1993); and "Early Works," Phoenix Art Museum, Phoenix, Arizona (1990). Philip's work is featured in public collections at the National Museum of American Art, Washington, D.C.; and the Museum of Modern Art, New York, New York. He is also the subject of a documentary entitled *An American Original, Philip Curtis*. The film has been shown throughout the United States and in Italy.

About his work, Phil says, "I take it pretty seriously, and I'm always pleased when people like it." When asked to describe himself, he says, "I try to contribute as much as I can in my own way."

Joel Coplin

Philip C. Curtis

Marc Jasper D'Ambrosi lists cycling, movies and "picking up [artist] John Battenberg at the airport" as his hobbies — seems Mr. Battenberg makes frequent trips to Phoenix. And when asked about any favorite foods, he quickly replies, "Anything at Razz's [Restaurant and Bar, in Scottsdale]."

Marc's education includes Weber State College, Ogden, Utah; Artist Foundry, Santa Monica, California; and Artists' and Sculptors' Foundry, Los Angeles, California. His work has appeared in many exhibitions, including the University of California, Fresno, California; Arizona Contemporary Artists, Tempe, Arizona; Scottsdale Center for the Arts, Scottsdale, Arizona; Dona Rose Gallery, Sun Valley, Idaho; Udinotti Galleries in San Francisco and Venice, California and Scottsdale; and Mega-Art Gallery, Soho, New York.

Marc and his work have also been the subject of features in numerous publications, including *The Arizona Republic, Los Angeles Times, PHOENIX Magazine* and *Southwest Art*.

John Dawson collects signed, first edition books, mostly mysteries. He loves old movies and says, "Ever since I was a kid, I've been a fan of Al Jolson. Oh, yeah, I love to cook, too. That's another hobby, one I do every day. I make all kinds of things, I find it really relaxing."

John's higher education includes Northern Illinois University, De Kalb, Illinois; University of New Mexico, Albuquerque, New Mexico; and Arizona State University, Tempe, Arizona. His work has appeared in solo exhibitions such as C.G. Rein Gallery, Scottsdale, Arizona, and in group exhibitions: America Art Now, Columbus Museum of Arts & Sciences, Columbus, Georgia; and Scottsdale Center for the Arts, Scottsdale.

"I started painting when I was very young, about twelve," he says. "This was the only thing I was ever interested in doing. My work tends to be humanist in nature: of mortality and immortality, the inability to communicate and how each individual is locked within himself, the dynamics of being a human being. I refer to them as stories without words."

Says John, "My mother told one time when I was younger, that someday I'd have to have a regular job and that I wouldn't be able to wear jeans and T-shirts. I'm still waiting for that to happen."

Marc Jasper D'Ambrosi

John Dawson

Karl Dowhie started out as a physics major. "But the Vietnam war interrupted," he says. "After being out of physics for four years, I found I could hardly count much less do quantum. I'd always done art as a kid. It was a great way to get out of class, being on the yearbook staff or decorating a stage play."

Karl's education includes a Bachelor of Fine Arts and Master of Fine Arts, both achieved at Arizona State University, Tempe, Arizona. His work has appeared in many exhibitions, including Scottsdale Center for the Arts, Scottsdale, Arizona; Phoenix Art Museum, Phoenix, Arizona; Adduci Fine Arts, Chicago, Illinois; and Anne Goodman Fine Arts, Marina del Rey, Los Angeles, California. Karl also has works in several collections, including Samaritan Health Services, Phoenix; First National Bank of Chicago, Chicago; and Art Center of Minnesota, Minneapolis, Minnesota.

As far as a preferred food, Karl says he goes for just about anything spicy. Lately, he's had a fondness for Caribbean foods. Had he not become an artist, he says, "I'd be a sailboat charter captain in the Caribbean. Everybody has one thing they'll probably never realize. That's my fantasy job."

About his work, he says, "I like to paint, I enjoy doing it. If people buy it, that's fine. If they don't, that's fine, too. Somebody will get it as a Christmas present."

John Edwards describes himself as taking everything very seriously "with a pinch of salt." He says it's never occurred to him to be anything but an artist. "I've always tried to give it up," he says, in jest, "but never managed it."

John's education includes Harrow and Central Schools of Art, London, England, where Adrian Berg, John Hoyland and Paul Huxley were among his tutors. He has traveled extensively throughout Europe and the United States. In 1996 he worked in studios in San Francisco and Phoenix and began a collaboration with John Battenberg on the European tour of Battenberg's work. John's work has appeared in solo exhibitions at Mayor Gallery and Christies Contemporary Art, both in London; and in group exhibitions at Spark Inc., Tokyo, Japan; Carone Gallery, Fort Lauderdale, Florida; and Gallery 33, Mossop Street, London, to list only a few. His work has also been the subject of features in *The London Times* and other publications.

John has a wide range of tastes in food "from Italian and French to Thai." Though English fare does not rank high with him, he says, "I do like a bit of English food, roast beef and Yorkshire pudding. Lynn Battenberg [wife of John Battenberg], incidentally makes the best... makes it better than my mother. Now that's something," he says, "I have to go to California to get roast beef."

Karl Dowhie

John Edwards

Bella Feldman once taught kindergarten, but chose an art career adventure, instead. She, like many artists, has little time for an actual hobby, saying most everything she does somehow relates to her work. When not in the studio creating, however, she spends some "spare" time teaching at the California College of Arts and Crafts in Oakland, California.

Bella's education includes Queens College, Queens, New York; and two degrees from San Jose State University, San Jose, California: Master of Arts and Master of Fine Arts. Her work has appeared in many exhibitions, including "Distinguished Woman Artist," Fresno Art Museum, Fresno, California (1996); Jan Baum Gallery, Los Angeles, California; Alternative Museum of New York, New York; Zaks Gallery, Chicago, Illinois; Foxley-Leach Gallery, Washington, D.C., and the University of Denver, Denver, Colorado.

Bella is also the recipient of many awards including the Distinguished Woman Artist of the Year, Fresno Art Museum, Fresno, California (1996); and two Visual Artist's Fellowships from the National Endowment for the Arts (1986, 1987).

Rudy Fernandez says he doesn't really have any hobbies. He collects art and travels, but says it's all related to art. "People talk about retiring," he says. "What would I do if I retired?" He does, however, love to cook. "I do some French and Italian. It's pretty eclectic, too," he says, adding that he also cooks what he calls traditional New Mexican as well as some dishes native to Southern Colorado.

Rudy's education includes a bachelor's degree in fine arts from the University of Colorado, Boulder, Colorado; and a master's degree in fine arts from Washington State University, Pullman, Washington. His work has been exhibited at many galleries, including the Bruce Kapson Gallery, Los Angeles, California; and the Museum of Fine Arts, Santa Fe, New Mexico. Solo showings include "Rudy Fernandez: Mixed Media Painting La Paza/Galeria Posada," Sacramento, California (1994); and "Nichos, Form and Function," Millicent Rogers Museum, Taos, New Mexico (1993).

"It changes," says Rudy about his work. "I'm guided by the art rather than me guiding the art. It's always been that way."

If he had not become an artist, Rudy says he might have taken two other roads, geologist or a lawyer. "I was accepted to law school at the University of Colorado and didn't go," he says. "I thought about it, but that's not what I wanted to do with my life. Me in a suit for the rest of my life? I don't think so."

Bella Feldman

Rudy Fernandez

Douglas Kent Hall says if he had not become an artist, "I suppose what I might have done otherwise, which is something I've been involved with, is movies. It combines two of the things I like, writing and art." He presently has to his writing credit novels, non-fiction, poetry and a little movie script writing.

When not writing or in his studio creating, Douglas has a passion for martial arts, teaching it as well at his martial arts school. His favorite foods include Italian, Mexican and Chinese. "I love pasta and I like the variations that happen in Oriental cooking. From Mexico, my favorite foods tend to be from the Yucatan that have to do with game. The cooking in Mexico is spectacular."

Douglas' education includes a Bachelor of Arts degree from Brigham Young University, Provo, Utah and a Master of Fine Arts from the University of Iowa, Iowa City, Iowa. His work has recently appeared in exhibitions at Bruce Kapson Gallery, Santa Monica, California; and Joy Tash Gallery, Scottsdale, Arizona. Additionally, his work is a part of collections such as those at Atlantic Richfield, Dallas, Texas and Los Angeles, California; the Chase Manhattan Bank, New York, New York; and Bibliotheque Nationale, Paris, France.

"I've always had this feeling your work should speak for itself," says Douglas about his work. "I'm very serious about the work I do. I do it because I think it's important."

James Havard believes he would probably be raising cattle somewhere had he not become an artist. He is fond of French food and when he's not in the studio creating he's probably tending to his garden or playing golf.

James' education includes Sam Houston State College, Huntsville, Texas, and Pennsylvania Academy of Fine Arts, Philadelphia, Pennsylvania. His work has appeared in solo exhibitions at Alan Stone Gallery, New York, New York; Lavignes-Bastille, Paris, France; and Janus Gallery, Los Angeles, California. Group exhibitions include Chicago International Art Exposition, Chicago, Illinois; Moos Gallery, Toronto, Ontario, Canada; and Abstrakter Illusionismus, America Haus, Frankfurt, Germany.

"It's a visual thing," says James about his work. "It's not deep intellectual things, although they do seem to be at times."

Douglas Kent Hall

James Havard

James Holmes says, "I knew from an early age I liked art. I was always drawing or building stuff. My brother is an artist, he's still quite an influence on me."

As an undergraduate at the University of Kansas, James says, "I thought I'd be in painting and drawing. I took a life drawing class (skeletal and muscular) and, oddly enough, it got me interested in sculpture. I went over to the sculpture department and never left."

James graduated from the University of Kansas, Lawrence, Kansas, with a bachelor's degree in fine arts and achieved a master's degree in fine arts from the School of the Art Institute of Chicago, Chicago, Illinois. His work has appeared in solo exhibitions at Cumberland Gallery, Nashville, Tennessee; Morgan Gallery, Kansas City, Missouri; and Pasadena City College Art Gallery, Pasadena, California. Group exhibitions include "Southwest 96," Santa Fe, New Mexico (1996); "Art Fair Seattle 96," Seattle, Washington (1996); and "International Shoebox Sculpture Show," University of Hawaii, Honolulu, Hawaii (1993).

James is an avid fly fisherman who has worked as a cabinet maker and a carpenter. He loves to cook and goes for Southwest food and barbecue. About his work he says, "Don't be afraid of the humor in it." About himself he says, "I really enjoy art, always have, and I can't wait to make something new."

Kevin Irvin plays golf when he's not in the studio creating and goes for the spiciness of Thai and Indian food. He originally thought about becoming an attorney or politician, but took the path of an artist instead.

"When you become an artist, it's really not even a career choice. It's sort of in you. It happened for me rather late. I grew up in a small town, I didn't know any artists. I went to college and took some classes, obviously always having a major interest, and I was fortunate enough to have two or three really great teachers. It was a small school where you got a lot of attention and things blossomed from there."

In addition to his bachelor's degree from Indiana State University, Evansville, Indiana, Kevin achieved a Master of Fine Arts from Arizona State University, Tempe, Arizona. His work has appeared in many exhibitions, including Horwitch Newman Gallery, Scottsdale, Arizona; Oklahoma State University, Bartlett Center, Stillwater, Oklahoma; Mary Moore Gallery, La Jolla, California; and Evansville Museum of Arts and Sciences, Evansville, Indiana.

"I work from personal experience," says Kevin. "It's very introspective and emotional."

James Holmes

Kevin Irvin

Kathryn Jacobi says she has little time for hobbies, but does say, "I love going to the opera and I'm a great walker. I spend a lot of my life walking when I'm not in the studio." Had she not become an artist, she says she would have been a writer of fiction and drama.

Kathryn is currently represented by several galleries, including Jan Baum Gallery, Los Angeles, California; Diane Farris Gallery, Vancouver, British Columbia, Canada; and Liasons Beaux Arts, Paris, France. Additionally, her work has been exhibited at PDX Gallery, Portland, Oregon; Kirsten Kjaers Museum, Skagan, Denmark; and among group exhibitions such as Lankershim Arts Center Gallery, "Survey of Contemporary American Prints," North Hollywood, California (1997); and Laband Art Gallery, Loyola Marymount University, "14th National Printmaking Exhibit," Los Angeles (1997).

About her work, Kathryn states, "While I have always considered myself a figurative artist, in the fall of 1990, I began a serious study of the painting techniques and materials of the Old Masters, especially those of the early Northern Renaissance... Inspired by their level of insight, skill and devotion, my task has been to create paintings which depict our contemporary reality in metaphoric images."

Kathryn Kain enjoys inline skating and cooking when not in the studio creating. "I collect cookbooks," she says. "I'm kind of into Mexican and Italian food." Kathryn goes for Santa Fe cooking, dishes with "lots of red chiles. And anything vegetarian with gourmet attributes."

About being an artist, she says, "It's the only thing I can imagine myself doing." She has, however, entertained thoughts of becoming an airline flight attendant, "so I could fly all over the world and do my art."

Kathryn's education includes a Bachelor of Fine Arts, honors degree in printmaking, from San Jose State University, San Jose, California; and a Master of Fine Arts in printmaking from San Francisco Art Institute, San Francisco, California. Her work has appeared in many exhibitions, including "Alumni Printmakers," University of California - Hayward, Hayward, California (1997); "Bay Area Printmaking," Sauder Visual Arts Center, Albrecht Gallery, Bluffton, California (1996); "A Woman's View," 20 North Gallery, Toledo, Ohio (1996).

"My work is inspired by my love of drawing and drawing natural things" says Kathryn. "Just to look at something and draw something is a wonderful thing."

Kathryn Jacobi

Kathryn Kain

Mayme Kratz likes movies and music when not painting. "Almost everything I do has something to do with my work or my vision," she adds. "One of the activities I really like is hiking and that has a direct influence on my work."

She describes herself as very quiet and tends to be introspective. "I like to be alone a lot of the time. And I can have fun, too."

When asked what she would be doing had she not become an artist, Mayme says, "I've been a self-employed artist for so many years that it's hard for me to even think about what else I'd do. I haven't thought of anything else since I was about fourteen." Prior to age fourteen, she says she entertained the idea of becoming a surgeon.

Mayme's art has appeared in solo exhibitions such as "Roots and Wings," Lisa Sette Gallery, Scottsdale, Arizona (1995); and in group exhibitions, including "House Sweet House," New Jersey Center for the Visual Arts, Summit, New Jersey (1994).

"I don't like to tell too much about my work, in the sense that I want people to interpret it for themselves," she says and later adds, "It's very involved with nature. It's very involved with being a human being and our interaction with nature and ourselves."

Earl Linderman collects rare books and has a fondness for 20th century literature. While he likes all different kinds of foods, he does admit to favoring Italian food. Had Earl not become an artist, he says, "I'd probably be a writer. I probably write novels, imaginative adventures and things of that nature."

Born in Endicott, New York, Earl's education includes the Albright Art School, Buffalo, New York and Pennsylvania State University, University Park, Pennsylvania, where he achieved both a master's and doctorate degrees. His work has been exhibited at such galleries as C.G. Rein Galleries, Scottsdale, Arizona; Vorpal Gallery, New York, New York; and Elaine Horwitch Galleries, Scottsdale, Arizona and Santa Fe, New Mexico, with selected collections at the Phoenix Art Museum, Phoenix, Arizona, and Arizona State University in Tempe, Arizona.

"I want people to see [my work] first as fine art," says Earl about his work, "and then to enjoy it for its other properties. It's narrative and whatever else can be discovered because it's a personal adventure."

Earl says of himself, "I'm always seeking the original, the unusual, the imaginative."

Mayme Kratz

Earl Linderman

Lyle London describes himself as a "well balanced person who enjoys a lot of different activities." He goes for Italian food, especially coastal Italian food. He counts catamaran sailing, golf and skiing as favorite activities. He is also an avid reader of fiction and scientific journals.

Lyle graduated *cum laude* from Dartmouth College, Hanover, New Hampshire, with a bachelor's degree in art. He studied with sculptor Varujan Boghosian and other artists — Larry Zox, Dimitri Hadzi, Robert Indiana, Jack Zajac — at Dartmouth. Zajac's style of biomorphic abstraction has had a lasting influence on his work. After several years of carving stone and practical experience in the art bronze foundry, Lyle began working primarily in metal. His work has been viewed at such exhibitions as "Lyle London & Laura Pope," Indigo Gallery, Portland, Oregon; "Sculpture for the Outdoors," Tory Folliard Gallery, Milwaukee, Wisconsin; and "The Best of Scottsdale," outdoor sculpture, Scottsdale Center for the Arts, Scottsdale, Arizona.

When asked what people should know about his work, Lyle says, "Only that they need to open the gates of perception."

Francisco Lopez (OCHOA) says, "Actually, I became an artist after I was doing something else. I'm a Ph.D. dropout from Georgetown [University, Washington, D.C.]. I was already thinking about changing to being an artist. I was in applied linguistics and when I went to take my comprehensives, I was hit on the head with a gun. They stole all my books that I'd taken to review for my comprehensives. So I decided then, this was a sign from heaven that I should go ahead and become an artist."

In addition to his degrees, Francisco's studies include printmaking/foundry at the Center for Creative Studies, Detroit, Michigan; sculpture and figure drawing at Summit Art Center, Summit, New Jersey; and clay modeling, an informal study with Marion Held, Montclair, New Jersey. His work has appeared in many exhibitions, including Greythorne Gallery, Scottsdale, Arizona; and Crashing Thunder Gallery, Gallup, New Mexico. Francisco's commissioned works include "Terra," a limestone sculpture, R.C. Gorman Collection, Taos, New Mexico; and "Hero," a welded steel sculpture, commissioned by the Hakone Open-Air Museum, on display on the grounds of the Utsukushi Ga-hara Open-Air Museum, Tokyo, Japan.

"There's no hidden meaning in my work," Francisco says. "It relates to family values, human emotions and relationships. It's very humanistic oriented."

Lyle London

Francisco Lopez (OCHOA)

Merrill Mahaffey says, "Skiing is my hobby in the winter and golf in the summer. I've been a cross-country skier and now I'm a high-speed cruiser. I like to go up on the lift and then go straight down. I figured out as I got older, the more I turned, the more tired I got. So it's easier just to go straight."

Merrill's education includes Mesa College, Grand Junction, Colorado; California College of Arts and Crafts, Oakland, California; and Arizona State University, Tempe, Arizona where he achieved a master's degree in fine arts. His solo exhibitions have appeared at such galleries as Suzanne Brown Gallery, Scottsdale, Arizona; Elaine Horwitch Galleries, Santa Fe, New Mexico; and Fishbach Gallery, New York, New York. Group exhibitions include Artists of America, Western Heritage Center, Denver, Colorado (1994); and Eiteljorg Invitational, Indianapolis, Indiana (1992). Merrill's work is also among collections at the Museum of American Art, Smithsonian Institute, Washington, D.C.

"I'm a very deliberate painter," he says. "Nothing on my canvas is accidental." Merrill describes himself as, "very active all the time. I'm somewhat athletic, that's the physical side. The brain side is that I'm constantly trying to learn about new things. I like ideas and I like science."

Michael Marlowe says cooking is a hobby and adds, "I love French food. I also have a seven-year-old, that takes up most of my other time." Additionally, he does quite a bit of set design work for theatre and film.

Michael's education includes a Bachelor of Fine Arts from Arizona State University, Tempe, Arizona; and a Master of Fine Arts in theatre set design, also from ASU. Michael's work has appeared at the Scottsdale Center for the Arts, Scottsdale, Arizona; Gallery Espace Timbaub, Paris, France; and the Elaine Horwitch Galleries, Scottsdale. Presently his work is showing at the Bentley Gallery, Scottsdale.

"Instead of approaching my work stylistically, from one work to another," he says, "there's always a real quick obvious follow through visually. My work is more connected through ideas... I think I work much more from ideas than I do from any sort of stylistic approach."

Merrill Mahaffey

Michael Marlowe

Mario Romero Mauricio was born in Mexico City, Mexico, and has spent years studying his craft, beginning with philosophy and art history. He then studied tapestry at the National Tapestry Workshop at the Instituto Nacional de Bellas Artes, Mexico City, and has learned the techniques of etching at various graphic arts workshops.

Mario's work has appeared in many exhibitions, including Polanco Gallery, San Francisco, California; Momentum Gallery, Los Angeles, California; Lafontsee Gallery, Grand Rapids, Michigan; Emergence Gallery, Morristown, New Jersey; and Museo Nacional de la Estampa, Salon de Miniestampa and Galeria Jose Maris Velasco, both in Mexico City. Recently, Mario's work was used as part of an advertising campaign for Jose Cuervo® Tequila.

About Mario's work, Agustin Martinez Castro writes, as translated by Aldo Picchi, "His work is a manifestation of a world rich in myths, each one of his images reveals a slice of his world."

Buck McCain may be camping or delving into one of his other hobbies, archeology and paleontology, when not in the studio creating. Actually, had he not become an artist, Buck says he would probably be an archeologist or paleontologist.

Buck's education includes Imperial Valley College, El Centro, California; the University of San Diego, San Diego, California; and Plasticas and University of Guadalajara Instituto de Artes, both in Guadalajara, Mexico. His work has appeared in a retrospective exhibit of painting and bronzes hosted by The Franklin Mint, Philadelphia, Pennsylvania (1994). Other work includes commissioned bronzes of Mary and Joseph, St. Thomas the Apostle Catholic Church, Tucson, Arizona (1992); and two sculptures exhibited in the U.S. Embassy in Madrid, Spain, for "The Art of the American West," Columbus quincentennial celebration. Buck has been featured in many publications including *Sunset, Southwest Art* and *Architectural Digest*.

"Although on a personal level my art is about a relationship with the spiritual," he says, "the meaning of my art is ultimately in the eyes of the viewer."

Mario Romero Mauricio

Buck McCain

Mark McDowell says, "I knew my second year in college I wanted to be an artist. I've always made things. My father is a carpenter; my uncle was a toy maker."

Raised in Pennsylvania, Mark includes among his favorite foods Sonoran Mexican, Italian and Thai. "I cook as well," he says, "a hobby, a pastime, a need. I do have a thing for food. One of the things about being an artist is that you have a zest for things and food would certainly be among them."

Mark has a bachelor's degree in fine arts from Pennsylvania State University, University Park, Pennsylvania. His work can presently be viewed at the Bentley Gallery, Scottsdale, Arizona and has been exhibited at Elaine Horwitch Galleries and Santa Fe East, Santa Fe, New Mexico. Group exhibitions include "Flower Paintings" (1995), Lizan - Tops Gallery, East Hampton, New York, and "The Eye of the Collector" (1994), Villanova University, Villanova, Pennsylvania.

"This is my vehicle to express my thoughts about the time in which I live," he says. "My paintings are of common objects, painted fairly representationally. Everything that I paint comes from some real thing that I've seen."

Mark describes himself as "a sort of a hands-on, experience-oriented person. I believe in hard work, diligence. If you work hard and stay true to your vision, you have an opportunity to succeed."

Ed Mell likes authentic Mexican food and food from El Salvador. He describes himself as "an average guy with a good job." When not in the studio, he's probably tinkering with his 1962, fawn beige Corvette. Ed and his Corvette participate in the Copper State 1000, an annual vintage car tour through Arizona.

On his artist career road, Ed has achieved an associate of arts degree from Phoenix College, Phoenix, Arizona; and a bachelor of fine arts degree from the Art Center College of Design, Los Angeles, California. His work has appeared at the Suzanne Brown Gallery, Scottsdale, Arizona; and the Rockwell Museum, Corning, New York. His "Brilliant Landscapes, Turbulent Skies; The Art of the Grand Canyon" was exhibited at the Museum of Northern Arizona, Flagstaff, Arizona.

"I'm going to be doing a mural for the Kartchner Caverns in southern Arizona, which is going to be a state park. I'll be working on it this summer," he says. "I also have a new book out this year which is called *Beyond the Visible Terrain, The Art of Ed Mell* (Northland Press).

Mark McDowell

Ed Mell

Jesús Bautista Moroles

knew he would be an artist when he was in the third grade. "I had great art teachers," he says. "My parents were very encouraging and sent me to private lessons."

Jesús holds a bachelor's degree in fine arts from North Texas State University, Denton, Texas. His work has appeared in exhibitions at Twentieth Century American Sculpture at The White House, Washington, D.C.; Long House Foundation, East Hampton, New York; and the Museum of Contemporary Art, Chicago, Illinois. Jesús also has to his credit a list of commissioned work for E.F. Hutton/CBS Plaza, New York; Desert Mountain Corporation, Scottsdale, Arizona; and the Birmingham Botanical Gardens, Birmingham, Alabama. Additional work appears in such public collections as the National Museum of American Art, Smithsonian, Washington, D.C.; and the Albuquerque Museum, Albuquerque, New Mexico.

"What I try to do is to combine man and nature," says Jesús, "to show man and nature working together. I pretty much let the work speak for itself."

When not in the studio, he plays golf. When it comes to any favorite foods, he says, "I like everything, sushi to paella to my Mom's menudo. I travel too much not to like everything."

Tom Ortega

is an avid runner, likes to hike and work on his backyard. He studied painting and drawing at North Texas State University in Denton, Texas, but ended up with an advertising degree from Texas Tech University, Lubbock, Texas. "I spent ten years as a writer with several ad agencies," he says, "and after ten years I decided I had held my artistic endeavors at bay long enough."

His work has appeared in such exhibitions as Triennial Sofia '96 International Exhibition of Painting, Sofia, Bulgaria; Expo Arte, Guadalajara, Mexico, with the Bentley Gallery of Scottsdale; Elaine Horwitch Gallery, Scottsdale; and Sally Sprout Gallery, Houston, Texas.

About his work, Tom says, "It's for sale."

"I've spent a long time exploring older parts of cities," he continues. "Those are the places where I feel comfortable. My work seems to be a lot about how time affects environment and place. It's not objective work, it's not representational in any way of these environments. What it does represent is that time has a way of layering and a way of creating images."

Jesús Bautista Moroles

Tom Ortega

Thomas A. Philabaum says
he might have been a Lutheran minister had he not become an artist. "When I was a kid, my family was very involved in the Lutheran church. In high school, I was considering going to seminary school, but then I saw the great art light and took that direction instead. My church has taken on a different form."

Tom has three graduate degrees; his work is in glass and ceramic. "My MFA is in ceramics," he says. "Glass has taught me to be a businessman, taught me patience. Glass has been a really good friend and teacher... I work with glass in both traditional and nontraditional methods. I paint on the glass, do a lot of oddball things to it. I treat the glass differently than some people would."

Tom's works have been exhibited in many solo showings and include National Glass, Phoenix Rising, Seattle, Washington (1995); A Gathering of Glass, Sable V, Wimberley, Texas (1994, 1995); and Glass Masters, Somerhill Gallery, Chapel Hill, North Carolina (1994). His work is also among collections at Arizona State University, Tempe, Arizona; and Icelandair Company, Reykjavik, Iceland.

"I fell in love with glass as an art material, not as a means of production or making a living," he says. "To me it was an idea and something I had to explore."

Howard Post grew up in Tucson,
Arizona, on a small ranch. "We raised horses and cattle for rodeo use," he says. "I've competed professionally in the rodeo, roping and bull dogging."

He became interested in art in the third grade. "My third grade teacher entered one of my drawings in a contest at the city newspaper and I won first prize and got my picture in the paper. I knew right then that this must be my calling and I have never wanted to do anything else."

Howard has a bachelor's and master's in the fine arts from the University of Arizona, Tucson, Arizona. His exhibitions include The Best of Southwest Art Traveling Exhibition (1994, 1995); Museum of History and Art, Salt Lake City, Utah; and Nabisco Invitational, East Hanover, New Jersey. Howard's work also appears in several public collections: AT&T, Morristown, New Jersey; The Smithsonian Institute, Washington, D.C.; and United Airlines, Denver, Colorado.

About his work, Howard says, "My aim is to portray the visual and emotional elements of a subject, to make it memorable for me."

Thomas A. Philabaum

Howard Post

Otto Rigan says his favorite food is, "Italian, hands down. The year I spent in Italy, there was one evening we went out and had Chinese. The rest of the year it was pasta." As for hobbies, Otto, like many artists, simply does not have the time. "What I do as an artist is completely consuming."

Otto's education includes the California College of Arts and Crafts, Oakland, California; and Academia de Belli Arti, Florence, Italy. His work has appeared in many exhibitions, including LUMINOUS ORDER, Deson-Saunders Gallery, Chicago, Illinois; Sena Galleries, Santa Fe, New Mexico; and Scottsdale Center for the Arts, Scottsdale, Arizona. Otto's work is also among many corporate collections, including Phoenix Newspapers, Inc., Phoenix, Arizona; Hotel Kansai, Osaka, Japan; Rockwell International, Seal Beach, California; and Ernst & Young, Los Angeles, California.

"It's not about monumentality," Otto says about his work, "it's about finding a relationship to nature." Had he not become an artist, he says, "Once in awhile when I wonder why I'm doing what I'm doing, I try to think of what the alternative would be and I can't. In college, I was extremely preoccupied with an interest in architecture. In some ways, I think making my sculptures is making my architecture."

Elias Rivera grew up in New York City. "It's a phenomenally fertile environment for a young artist to grow up in," he says. "It would have been, for me, an enormous vacuum to not be able to fulfill this need I have." Had Elias not become an artist, he might have explored the art of cabinet making. He knew, however, from an early age he was to be an artist. As a child, Elias was confined to bed because of an illness. His mother gave him some clay to pass the time. "From that moment on, I knew I was going to be an artist," he says.

Elias' work has appeared in solo exhibitions, including Riva Yares Gallery, "Visions of Solola," Santa Fe, New Mexico; Cacciola Gallery, New York, New York; and Partners Gallery, "Hispanic Invitation Show," Bethesda, Maryland. His work is also among public collections at the Albuquerque Museum of Fine Arts, Albuquerque, New Mexico; and the Metropolitan Museum of Art, New York.

Elias says his work honors the human spirit in man. "I've always been geared to working class people." About himself he says, "I feel the responsibility to be devotional in my work because I have received such phenomenally beautiful moments in the world of art, especially painting. Painting is my devotion."

Otto Rigan

Elias Rivera

Gustavo Ramos Rivera enjoys walking and bicycling when not in the studio creating. He also loves food. "Don't we all?" he asks. "I enjoy spicy, but low-fat foods. World cuisine, basic foods." And, had he not become an artist, he says, "I'd make a good gardener. I enjoy gardening."

Gustavo has learned his artistic craft on his own. His works have appeared in many exhibitions, including solo showings at John Berggruen Gallery, San Francisco, California; Wilfried Von Gunter Galerie, Thun, Switzerland; and Arte Actual Mexicano, Monterrey Nuevo Leon, Mexico. Group exhibitions include Galerie Rahn, Zurich, Switzerland; and "The Painted Monotype," Joan Prats Gallery, New York, New York.

Gustavo has also been the subject of features in several publications, such as "Demonstrating the Ways of Art," *San Francisco Chronicle*, San Francisco, California. Wrote Eric Hellman in *Artweek*, in 1979, "...the emotional and visual intensity of colors and their relationships seems to represent the primary thrust of Rivera's work. Rivera is not a radical visionary; he is, however, willing to paint directly from the heart."

Mel Roman says he'd probably be a film maker had he not become an artist. He loves Chinese and Italian food, music (jazz) and, of course, movies. "I see almost every movie, good or bad."

When asked to describe himself, Mel says, "I'm an artist and psychologist. I was a professor at a medical school for many years. I've been sort of two-headed most of my life, a shrink and an artist. One's for listening, the other's for speaking. Right now, I'm working full-time on my art."

Mel's education includes City College of New York and New York University, New York. He has also studied with Hans Huffman and Robert Mallary. His work has been exhibited at the Bentley Gallery, Scottsdale, Arizona; Allene Lapides, Santa Fe, New Mexico; Tucson Museum Fine Arts, Tucson, Arizona; and Scottsdale Center for the Arts, Scottsdale, Arizona. Among the public and corporate collections, Mel lists the City of Scottsdale in Arizona; LBJ Museum, Austin, Texas; and the Martin Wither Kemp Museum, Atlanta, Georgia.

"Most of my work is psychologically oriented," says Mel. "It's conceptual, both in terms of psychological issues and political issues."

Gustavo Ramos Rivera

Mel Roman

Paul Sarkisian knew from an early age he was going to be an artist. He is a vegetarian, professing a preference for "greens," and when not in his studio creating, he says he can be found at a "nice coffee shop where there are lots of nice people, the Aztec Cafe."

Paul's education includes The School of the Art Institute of Chicago, Chicago, Illinois; Otis Art Institute, Los Angeles, California; and Mexico City College, Mexico City, Mexico. His work has appeared in solo exhibitions at Tomasula Gallery, Union County College, Cranford, New Jersey; Aspen Center for Visual Arts: Southwest Artists Series, Aspen, Colorado; and Fendrick Gallery, Washington, D.C.

His group exhibitions include "The Allure of Illusionism: Trompe L'Oeil — In Contemporary American Painting," Nora Eccles Harrison Museum of Art, Utah State University, Logan, Utah (1992); and "Directors Invitation," Helen B. Murray Gallery, Tacoma Art Museum, Tacoma, Washington (1988). Paul's work is also among public collections at the Art Institute of Chicago; Metropolitan Museum of Art, New York, New York; and the Museum of Modern Art, Vienna, Austria to name only a few.

Bill Schenck, in addition to being an artist, says, "For the last twenty-two years, I also have been involved with collecting and restoring prehistoric Southwestern pottery." He also deals in antique Navajo textiles and antique Apache baskets. "I travel extensively to auctions. I also rodeo," he adds. "In between all that, I build spectacular houses." Plus, Bill is a devoted movie buff and collects Donald Duck comic books.

Bill's education includes Columbus College of Art and Design, Columbus, Ohio; and a Bachelor of Fine Arts from Kansas City Art Institute, Kansas City, Missouri. His work has appeared in many exhibitions, including Susan Duval Gallery, Aspen, Colorado; Wyoming State Museum, Cheyenne, Wyoming; Scottsdale Center for the Arts, Scottsdale, Arizona; Louis K. Meisel Gallery, New York, New York; and Alberta College Art Gallery, Calgary, Alberta, Canada.

When asked what people should know about his work, Bill replies, "They should learn a lot about it; it is historically significant." Bill, along with Luis Jimenez, Bob Wade and Fritz Scholder, are what he calls the "founding fathers of a whole new way of looking at regional Western imagery, pop Western if you will."

Paul Sarkisian

Bill Schenck

Fritz Scholder is a prolific, internationally acclaimed sculptor and painter. His education includes the University of Wisconsin, Superior, Wisconsin; a Bachelor of Arts from Sacramento State University, Sacramento, California; and Master of Fine Arts from the University of Arizona, Tucson, Arizona.

His work has appeared in many exhibitions, including "Fritz Scholder, Thirty Years of Sculpture," Arizona State University, Tempe, Arizona; Riva Yares Gallery, Santa Fe, New Mexico; Alexander Gallery, New York, New York; Massachusetts Institute of Technology, Cambridge, Massachusetts; Art Gallery of Ontario, Toronto, Canada; Bibliotheque Nationale, Paris, France.

Fritz has been the subject of eight books, two PBS documentaries as well as a listing in both *Who's Who in America* and *Who's Who in the World*. He has been artist in residence at Dartmouth College, the University of Southern California and the American University in Washington, D.C. Fritz has received fellowships from the Whitney Foundation, Rockefeller Foundation, Ford Foundation and the American Academy of Arts and Letters. Among his numerous awards, is recognition from the Salon d'Automne in Paris and Intergrafkis in Berlin.

Kevin Sloan says when viewing his work, people need to know it's okay to "feel" their way through it. "You don't necessarily have to think your way through it," he says. "My paintings are very visually oriented. They're about things of the world as they relate to each other. It's a feeling sort of thing."

Kevin was raised in the Midwest and as an early teen considered becoming an architect. Though he took a different path, he says, "I think it's probably one of the most significant art forms in the culture. Often that's what's really left to look back upon, the buildings, the layout of cities."

He has achieved a bachelor of fine arts in painting from Tyler School of Art, Temple University, Philadelphia, Pennsylvania; and a master of fine arts in painting from the University of Arizona, Tucson, Arizona. His work has appeared in many solo and group exhibitions including the Lisa Sette Gallery, Scottsdale, Arizona; Galerie Simonne Stern, New Orleans, Louisiana; and Lucky Street Gallery, Key West, Florida. Kevin's paintings are also part of several public collections including Chase Manhattan Bank, New York, New York; and The Israel Museum, Jerusalem, Israel.

Kevin bikes, swims, has a thing for German chocolate cake and describes himself as being "excited all the time about the world I'm living in."

Fritz Scholder

Kevin Sloan

Joe Willie Smith has been an artist all his life. "Ever since I was a kid, I actually made money doing artwork. I come from a very poor family. My mom worked as a housecleaning woman for the University of Wisconsin, and she would bring home these old white plates. I would paint animals and things on them. She would take them back and sell them to the professors for $5 apiece and give me the money for art supplies. I learned early I could make money doing this."

His solo exhibitions include Hava Java, Phoenix, Arizona; Ethnic Artifacts, Scottsdale, Arizona; and The Downtown Gallery, Phoenix. Joe's work also appears in such group exhibitions as Nelson Art Museum, Arizona Artists Here and Now, Arizona State University, Tempe, Arizona; La Phoeniquere, Mars Art Space, Phoenix; Arizona State Capitol, Artists of the Black Community; and at Symphony Hall, Phoenix.

"My work tends to be centered around a lot of personal statements and, many times, social statements," he says. "Sometimes it's aggressive, other [times] it's more subtle. I work with wood a lot and found objects. I tend to always use texture and distressed wood in some way."

Mark Spencer, being a history buff, says he would have probably gone into archaeology or architecture had he not become an artist.

Mark's education includes the School of the Museum of Fine Arts, Boston. His work has appeared in many exhibitions, including Gerald Peters Gallery, Santa Fe, New Mexico; Boston Center for the Arts and Copley Society Gallery, both in Boston; Foundations Gallery, New York, New York; and the MGM Grand Gallery, Las Vegas, Nevada. Mark's work is also among collections at the Museum of Fine Arts, Santa Fe; Boston Public Library, Boston; and Dartmouth College, Hanover, New Hampshire, to list only a few.

Various publications have featured Mark and his work, including *Artspace, Albuquerque Journal* and *Santa Fe Art* by Simone Ellis, Crescent Books (1993).

In a statement about his work, Mark says, "My art is about transformation. It's about rites of passage. It's about the ineffable mystery underlying what we take for granted. It's about the constant, unrelenting change and growth of our time. It's about the Divine in the mundane."

Joe Willie Smith

Mark Spencer

Beth Ames Swartz states, "It seems as if I was born to make art." And to her credit she has enjoyed over 50 solo art exhibitions including a showing at The Jewish Museum in New York City.

Beth's education includes a Bachelor of Science from Cornell University, Ithaca, New York; and a Master of Arts from New York University in New York. Currently, she is represented by the E.M. Donahue Gallery in New York and the Joy Tash Gallery in Scottsdale, Arizona. Other exhibitions of her work have been held at the Elaine Horwitch Galleries, Scottsdale; ACA Galleries, New York; Tilden/Folley, New Orleans, Louisiana; and Frank Marino, New York.

Beth's work also appears in collections at the National Museum of American Art at the Smithsonian, Washington, D.C.; Denver Art Museum, Denver, Colorado; Phoenix Art Museum, Phoenix, Arizona; as well as among corporate collections at IBM, Phelps Dodge and Phoenix Sky Harbor International Airport, Phoenix. A book on her work, *Connecting: The Art of Beth Ames Swartz,* (Northland Press, Ltd.) was published in 1984.

When not in her studio creating, Beth says she enjoys travel, reading and hiking.

Aung Aung Taik was born and raised in Rangoon (now known as Yangon), Burma. During the last year of his boarding school education, he knew he would be an artist. "When you're a kid and you know you're good at painting, you like to paint. But at the same time your parents are guiding you to be this and that. But in the end, the true fate prevails. I've gone through so many things to arrive at this point."

Aung Aung's education includes the State Academy of Art in Rangoon and private lessons from two of Burma's leading artists, U Ba Kyi and U Ngwe Gaing. After immigrating to the United States in 1972, he continued his studies at the San Francisco Art Institute and later taught at De Young Museum Art School, San Francisco, California. His work has appeared in many exhibitions, including Washington Square Gallery, Palace of Fine Arts and Fort Mason Art Center, all in San Francisco.

"I paint abstracts, realistic abstracts," he says. "I reflect the time that is to come, but I'm not pinpointing what it is." Aung Aung is also the author of an autobiographical novel, *Visions of Shwedagon,* White Lotus, Bangkok, Thailand (1989) and a cookbook, *Under the Golden Pagoda: The Best of Burmese Cuisine,* Chronicle Books (1993).

Beth Ames Swartz

Aung Aung Taik

Bob "Daddy-O" Wade says his Daddy-O tag is "an old college name. I got it when I came here to college, in Austin, back in 1961. I had come out of a custom car, hot rod background out of El Paso. I had long hair and that sort of stuff and I got the 'Daddy-O' moniker. A lot of friends still call me that."

Bob's education includes a bachelor's degree in fine arts from the University of Texas, Austin, Texas; and a master's degree in fine arts from the University of California, Berkeley, California. His work has appeared in solo exhibitions, including William Campbell Contemporary Art, Fort Worth, Texas; and Stremmel Gallery, Reno, Nevada. Group showings include "HISTORY of Texas Sculpture," University of Texas, Austin, Texas; "Wild West Show," Alberta College of Art, Calgary, Alberta, Canada; and the 10th Paris Biennale, National Museum of Modern Art, Paris, France.

It's not surprising, after all, that Bob "Daddy-O" Wade has a turquoise and white '57 Chevy to tinker with now and then. Incidentally, he credits his custom car background for an understanding and familiarity with the techniques, procedures and such involved with the production of his sculptures. Bob also collects old vintage photos and postcards, which he also uses in his work.

Edward "Rusty" Walker has a black belt in karate — Okinawan Shuri-ru. "When I was younger, I lived in Okinawa for 2 1/2 years [he comes from a military background]. The mental training with martial arts helps my painting and my normal life situations and getting through stress. Meditation focuses you and centers you."

"I always knew I would be an artist," he says. "The first thing I drew were boxers. I was interested in boxing as a kid. It's sort of the yin and yang when you think about it — sports and art — they're different, almost opposites."

Rusty has a bachelor's, a master's and a doctorate degree, and served in the Air Force. He painted full time in the San Francisco area until 1985. And after a couple of trips to Europe, "I wrote a book on painting, *Transparent Watercolor* (Northlight, 1987). I paint different cultures and people, landscapes, seascapes, different environments."

"When I saw the light of the Southwest — Taos, the Pueblos, Monument Valley and Canyon de Chelly — I was quite struck by the light, like a lot of painters are. It is so incredibly different from California or Europe."

Rusty's work is presently exhibited at the C.G. Rein Gallery, Scottsdale, Arizona. His work is also in the permanent collections of the San Francisco Museum of Modern Art, San Francisco, California.

Bob "Daddy-O" Wade

Rusty Walker

Masoud Yasami refers to himself as "the old man and the sea. Every summer for sixteen years, I have lived on a 34-foot sailboat at Marina del Rey. That's what I do in the summers, fish and sail."

About his work, Masoud says, "My work is all about balance. The water, the earth. Those two are really dynamic texture differences, experiences. One you're on solid footing and the other you are not. So that right there creates a nice balance and that creates some drama in my work."

Masoud's education includes degrees from the University of California, Berkeley, California; Oregon State University, Corvallis, Oregon; and Arizona State University, Tempe, Arizona. His work has appeared in exhibitions such as *Trompe L'oeil*: the Magic of Deception, Muckenthaler Center for the Arts, Fullerton California. Other exhibitions include the Elaine Horwitch Galleries, Scottsdale, Arizona and the Scottsdale Center for the Arts, Scottsdale. His work is also part of several public collections including the University of Wisconsin, Madison, Wisconsin, and Tucson Museum of Art, Tucson, Arizona.

Masoud describes himself as a perfectionist, and says, "I would be classified as an artisan, from the old school. I love what I do."

Masoud Yasami

Artist Image Index

Donald
Downes has written about restaurants, food and people since 1989. His work has appeared in many publications, including *PHOE-NIX Magazine, Scottsdale Magazine, Scottsdale Progress Tribune, Frequent Flyer, Chile Pepper, Food & Wine* and *USA Today.* Currently, Donald writes monthly restaurant columns for *Today's Arizona Woman, WHERE Phoenix/Scottsdale* and *PHX Downtown.* He holds a Culinary Arts & Sciences and Restaurant Management degree from the Scottsdale Culinary Institute, Scottsdale, Arizona, and has cooked professionally in resort kitchens.

To order additional copies of **Pleasures of the Palettes,** call Golden West Publishers:
1-800-658-5830 or 602-265-4392